Property Tax Lien Foreclosure

Forms and Procedures

William A. Campbell

Sixth Edition 2003

Access Free Foreclosure Forms

Purchase of this book includes FREE access to forms used when foreclosing on real property using the mortgage-style foreclosure process. The forms are interactive (in Microsoft Word format) and designed to be saved as templates to use repeatedly.

Electronic download available

Visit the URL below to access and download your forms today: **sog.unc.edu/pubs/9781560114598**

For information about other publications and resources from the UNC School of Government, visit **sog.unc.edu**.

UNC SCHOOL OF GOVERNMENT

THE UNIVERSITY of NORTH CAROLINA at CHAPEL HILL

CONTENTS

1   FORMS AND PROCEDURES FOR A FORECLOSURE UNDER G.S. 105-374

COMPROMISE   66

CERTIFICATE OF TAXES DUE   67

NOTICE OF SALE   69

PLACING A SIGN ON THE PROPERTY   71

NOTICE OF SALE TO OWNER   72

REPORT OF SALE   72

UPSET BIDS   73

ASSIGNMENT OF BID   75

CONFIRMATION   77

JUDGMENT OF CONFIRMATION   78

COMMISSIONER'S DEED   80

COMMISSIONER'S FINAL REPORT   82

MEMORANDUM TO TAX OFFICES   84

2   FORMS AND PROCEDURES FOR AN *IN REM* FORECLOSURE UNDER G.S. 105-375

INTRODUCTION   87

FORECLOSURE HISTORY   88

LETTER TO LISTING TAXPAYER, CURRENT OWNER, AND LIENHOLDERS   90

3   POST-SALE MATTERS

PREFACE

This revision of the foreclosure form book (fifth edition) published by the Institute of Government in 1999 reflects changes in forms resulting from new and amended statutes and judicial decisions. Chapter 1 contains forms for use in the mortgage type of foreclosure provided for in G.S. 105-374; Chapter 2 contains forms for use in the *in rem* foreclosure provided for in G.S. 105-375; and Chapter 3 discusses the procedures to be followed when a taxing unit becomes the purchaser of property at a foreclosure sale. The forms are arranged in the sequence in which they would normally be used in a typical foreclosure action.

Chapel Hill
2003

1

FORMS AND PROCEDURES FOR A FORECLOSURE UNDER G.S. 105-374

FORMS AND PROCEDURES FOR A FORECLOSURE UNDER G.S. 105-374

INTRODUCTION

Foreclosure of the tax lien on real property by means of an action in the nature of a mortgage foreclosure pursuant to G.S. 105-374 is a civil action with all the requirements and characteristics of such an action. The lien being foreclosed is created by G.S. 105-355(a); it includes both the taxes on the land itself, plus interest and any late-listing penalties, and the taxes on all personal property—except registered motor vehicles— owned by the owner of the land, plus interest and penalties.[1] The priority of this lien is established by G.S. 105-356(a) and it is superior to all other liens and claims regardless of when they attached.[2] The forms in this book are designed for foreclosing the property tax lien, but they may be adapted for foreclosing the liens of special assessments by adding the appropriate allegations.[3]

As expensive and time-consuming as a foreclosure action may be in many cases, it serves two important purposes in addition to collecting the delinquent taxes on the property: it clears the title to the property, and it places the property back on the active tax rolls by transferring it to a new owner who will be responsible for the taxes.

PRE-FORECLOSURE CHECKLIST

Because a foreclosure is so expensive and complex, it should be the remedy of last resort for enforced collection. Before turning the delinquent account over to an attorney for foreclosure, the tax collector should have

---

1. For a discussion of the tax lien on real property, see W. CAMPBELL, PROPERTY TAX COLLECTION IN NORTH CAROLINA (4th ed. 1998), ch. V; the discussion of personal property taxes that are part of the lien on real property is at p. 131.

2. For a discussion of the lien priority, see *id.* 74–76.

3. *See* N.C. GEN. STAT. § 105-374(g).

FORM 1. PRE-FORECLOSURE CHECKLIST

1. Location of owner
   - ☐ A. Telephone book
   - ☐ B. City and suburban directories
   - ☐ C. Tax records
   - ☐ D. City Revenue/Assessments Department records
   - ☐ E. Neighbors of property owner
   - ☐ F. Owners of property next to subject property
   - ☐ G. N.C. secretary of state (for address or registered agent, if a corporation)
   - ☐ H. N.C. Department of Revenue [G.S. 105-289(e)]
   - ☐ I. Postal service forwarding or address-correction request
   - ☐ J. Credit Bureau, Merchants Association, law enforcement, bankruptcy/wage-earner office, or other source
   - ☐ K. Internet search

2. Attempts to use remedies other than foreclosure:
   - ☐ A. Demand letter(s)
   - B. Garnishment
       - ☐ 1. Employment (adjoining counties if not local)
       - ☐ 2. Bank account
       - ☐ 3. Other (debts, bonds, stocks, or money due taxpayer from third party)
   - C. Levy on personal property
       - ☐ 1. Automobile
       - ☐ 2. Other

attempted to collect the taxes by means of levy or attachment and garnishment. Form 1 is intended to make sure that the collector has made this effort. Even if it turns out that the remedies against personal property cannot be used successfully, use of the checklist may develop valuable information about the identity and address of the owner of the property.

TAX-LISTING AND PAYMENT RECORD

After delinquent accounts have been turned over to the attorney for collection, the first task is to obtain all of the information necessary for determining the status of the accounts and for taking formal action. That information must be obtained from the official files of the taxing unit. Form 2 provides a means for accumulating that information in a single record that, once prepared, will be immediately accessible to the attorney.

FORM 2. TAX-LISTING AND PAYMENT RECORD

Name of listing owner for ____________ : ____________________________

Owner's address: ____________________________________

Address of property: ____________________________________

Description: [insert a legal description of the property involved].

1 Year	2 Listed by	3 Taxes on Parcel	4 Pers. Prop. Taxes	5 Date Paid	6 Special Assess- ments	7 Date Paid
1993						
1994						
1995						
1996						
1997						
1998						
1999						
2000						
2001						
2002						

The record may be in the form of either a card or a sheet, and it should be compiled by the tax collector or by the attorney with the tax collector's help. The record gives the attorney a history of tax payments for the property involved during the preceding ten years and also a history of the property's ownership. A separate sheet should be prepared for each parcel of land against which a lien is being foreclosed.

The following comments apply to the indicated columns on Form 2.

1. In this column should be listed the year in which the taxes became due. G.S. 105-378 provides that no action for the enforced collection of taxes may be taken more than ten years after the taxes became due. The statute does, however, appear to be a true statute of limitations, which must be pleaded.

2. The name of the person who listed the taxes for each of the years involved and the spouse—if any—should be ascertained because each of these persons will be a necessary party to the foreclosure action.

3. The amount of the taxes due on the real property itself should be listed in this column.

4. All delinquent personal property taxes—except those on
    registered motor vehicles—should be listed in this column because
    G.S. 105-355(a) provides that they constitute a lien on the real
    property of the taxpayer, and the taxing unit would want the amount
    of these taxes included in the total for which foreclosure is being
    instituted.

5. If the personal property taxes have been paid, they are of no further
    interest and should not be included in the complaint. If a particular
    pattern of payment or nonpayment appears, however, the attorney
    may wish to ask the tax collector about the reasons for the pattern.

6. The liens for any delinquent special assessments should be included
    in the complaint and foreclosed along with the taxes.

7. Any assessments that have been paid are of no further interest and
    should not be included in the complaint.

LETTER TO OWNER

No one would suggest that the attorney, when accounts are assigned to
him or to her, should immediately institute foreclosure actions to collect
those accounts. Steps taken before a foreclosure action is begun often suc-
ceed in inducing payment of delinquent accounts. The letter set out in
Form 3 (not required by statute) is intended to make the taxpayer aware
that his account has been turned over to an attorney for formal action;
threatened sale of a person's property often brings payment.

The tax collector may have already sent a letter to the taxpayer just
before the delinquent accounts were turned over to the attorney; if so, the
attorney must judge whether another letter would be useful.

Letters of this kind are usually more effective when prepared on the
attorney's own stationery than when typed on the taxing unit's letterhead.

LETTER TO LIENHOLDER

The letter to the lienholder, set out in Form 4, has the same purpose as
the letter to the owner. Often lienholders will not know that the owner is
delinquent in paying taxes, but if informed of this fact, they may pay the
taxes in order to protect their interests when faced with the threat of foreclosure. Again, no statute requires that such a letter be sent, but experi-
ence has shown that this letter, like the one to the owner, frequently
brings about payment without formal action.

Unfortunately, if the taxpayer owes taxes on more than one parcel of
real property, plus personal property taxes, the amount to be inserted in
the "Taxes and Interest Due" column will not be the same in this letter
as it is in the letter to the owner set out in Form 3. G.S. 105-362(b)(1)b

FORM 3. **LETTER TO OWNER**

Dear __________________________:

The records of ________________ [City or County of __________________]
show that taxes on your property for the years listed below and in the amounts designated are past
due and unpaid. These delinquent taxes have been placed in my hands, as attorney, with instructions to collect them without delay or to institute a suit to foreclose and sell the real estate described
below on which these taxes are liens.

Year	Amount (including interest)
______	$ __________________
______	$ __________________
Total taxes and interest due	$ __________________

Additional interest will be added to the above amounts as provided by law if payment is not
made before the first day of next month. The taxes, plus all interest and costs that may accrue, constitute a first lien on the following real estate:

[description of real estate].

Unless these taxes are paid or a satisfactory arrangement is made with regard to payment
before _____________________________, I am instructed to institute suit without further
notice. I hope that you will take care of this matter within the time indicated and avoid having to
pay additional costs or having your property sold.

If you no longer own this real estate, please tell me who is responsible for paying the taxes
thereon.

Very truly yours,

Attorney for [City]

[County] of ___________________________________

provides that any interested party other than the owner can obtain the
discharge of the lien of the taxes on a particular piece of real estate by
paying the taxes due on that property (with interest and penalties) "plus
a proportionate part of personal property taxes owed by the listing taxpayer for the same year." On the other hand, the listing taxpayer, to
secure the release of the lien on this property, would have to pay the
amount of the taxes on the particular parcel of real estate (with interest
and penalties) and the full amount of his or her personal property taxes
(with interest and penalties).

This distinction and the different methods for computing the amounts necessary to secure the release of the lien for a particular parcel of real estate are demonstrated in the following illustration.

Suppose the taxpayer lists two parcels of real property, Tract A assessed at $30,000 and Tract B assessed at $20,000. He also lists personal property assessed at $5,000. The unit's tax rate is $1 per $100 of valuation. The taxpayer's bill is computed as follows:

Real Property:	
Tract A, $30,000—at $1 per $100	$300.00
Tract B, $20,000—at $1 per $100	200.00
Personal Property:	
$5,000—at $1 per $100	<u>50.00</u>
Total Tax	$550.00

For purposes of illustration, assume that the taxpayer desires to obtain a release of Tract B from the lien of the tax in May following the due date. The interest at that point will be $15.00 on the tax imposed on Tract A, $10.00 on Tract B, and $2.50 on the personal property. If the taxpayer (or the taxpayer's representative) is to obtain the release, the amount of the payment will be computed as follows:

Principal amount of tax levied against Tract B, plus interest	$210.00
All taxes levied against taxpayer's personal property, plus interest	<u>52.50</u>
Total to be paid in order to release Tract B	$262.50

If, on the other hand, someone other than the taxpayer has an interest in Tract B and tenders the payment required to obtain the release, it will be computed as follows:

Principal amount of tax levied against Tract B, plus interest	$210.00
Proportionate part (40%) of taxes levied against taxpayer's personal property	<u>21.00</u>
Total to be paid in order to release Tract B	$231.00

The first computation needs no explanation, but in the second computation—that is, the one in which someone other than the taxpayer is making the payment—the method for fixing the proportionate part of the personal property tax at 40 percent should be explained. Directions for determining this figure are set out in G.S. 105-362(b)(1)b: "The proportionate part shall be a percentage of the personal property taxes equal

FORM 4. LETTER TO LIENHOLDER

Dear _______________________________:

The records in the office of the Register of Deeds [Clerk of the Superior Court] of _______________________ County reveal that by virtue of a deed of trust [judgment, or lien] recorded in Book ________, page ____, you may be interested in real estate located in _______________________ Township, _______________________ County, and described as follows:

[description].

There have been placed in my hands for collection or foreclosure without further delay delinquent taxes that are liens upon the above described property as follows:

Year   Amount (including interest)

________ $ _______________________

________ $ _______________________

Total taxes and interest due $ _______________________

Additional interest will be added to the taxes for each month they remain unpaid.

This letter is written to give you an opportunity to protect your interest in the above property by paying the delinquent taxes (which will thereby give you a lien on the property in the amount of the taxes paid; see G.S. 105-386) if you care to do so. Unless either payment is made by _______________________ or a satisfactory arrangement for payment is made by that date, it will be my duty to proceed with suit to foreclose this property without further notice, and the foreclosure sale will be free and clear of your lien.

I hope you will take care of this matter by the date indicated and avoid additional interest and costs.

Very truly yours,

____

Attorney for [City]

[County] of _______________________________

to the percentage of the total assessed valuation of the taxpayer's real property in the taxing unit represented by the assessed valuation of the parcel or parcels sought to be released." In the example, the taxpayer listed two parcels of land—Tract A assessed at $30,000 and Tract B assessed at $20,000—for a total real estate assessment of $50,000. The 40 percent figure is arrived at by determining that $20,000 represents 40 percent of the total assessed value of the owner's land, $50,000.

FORM 5. TITLE ABSTRACT

The form might best be prepared on three separate sheets of paper: **Sheet 1:** This sheet should be virtually identical to Form 2, Tax-Listing and Payment Record, although the amount of taxes need not be included. It gives the title examiner a start on the chain of title and contains a complete legal description of the property; see Form 2 for a model. **Sheets 2 and 3:** Here each section may be expanded as desired.

	Record Owner	Date of Acquisition	Book	Page
As of January 1, _______	_____	_____________	_______	_______
As of January 1, _______	_____	_____________	_______	_______
As of January 1, _______	_____	_____________	_______	_______

Record of Deeds of Trust and Mortgages

1. Deed of trust from ______________ to ______________, trustee for

    ____. Amount $______________.

    Filed ______________ in Book _______, page _______.

2. Deed of trust from ______________ to ______________, trustee for

    ____. Amount $______________.

    Filed ______________ in Book _______, page _______.

Record of Judgments

1. Judgment Docket Book _______, page _______, docketed __________, in the amount
    of $______________, plus interest and costs;

    Plaintiff v. ______________________________, Defendant.

2. Judgment Docket Book _______, page _______, docketed __________, in the amount
    of $______________, plus interest and costs;

    Plaintiff v. ______________________________, Defendant.

Record of Liens

1. State liens: [describe them].
2. Federal liens: [describe them].
3. Liens of other local units: [describe them].
4. Liens of materialmen, etc.: [describe them].

Record of Names and Addresses of Necessary Parties Defendant

Name	Address	Comments
_______________	_________________	_________________
_______________	_________________	_________________

Comments and Notes

Checked for foreclosure action on _______ day of ______________, _______.

____

Attorney

TITLE ABSTRACT

After sufficient time has elapsed to assure the attorney that letters and other reminders have not induced payment, he should begin taking steps toward foreclosure.

Form 5 is a suggested instrument for gathering the information necessary to bring suit and provide the attorney with the names of all interested parties, the legal description of the property, and any defects in the chain of title that might affect the tax title and might be cured in the foreclosure action.

The description of the property must be checked with great care. The attorney should note anything that would render a foreclosure judgment irregular or ineffective to convey clear title.

The attorney must be sure to list all necessary parties as provided in G.S. 105-374(c):

1. the listing taxpayer;
2. the listing taxpayer's spouse;
3. the current owner of the property;
4. all other taxing units having tax liens against the property;
5. all other lienholders of record; and
6. all persons who would be entitled to be made parties to a court action (in which no deficiency judgment is sought) to foreclose a mortgage on such property.

This list must include trustees and beneficiaries in deeds of trust, judgment creditors and lienholders, and all former owners of the property who conveyed it by general warranty deed after the tax lien being foreclosed attached, whether or not there are any delinquent taxes in the names of those owners. *Overstreet v. City of Raleigh*, 75 N.C. App. 351, 330 S.E.2d 643 (1985), held that the taxing unit has no duty to ascertain whether any person claims title to the property through adverse possession and, if so, to serve that person.

In considering the matter of necessary parties, a review of three North Carolina Supreme Court decisions is instructive. In *Orange County v. Wilson*, 202 N.C. 424, 163 S.E. 113 (1932), the court indicated that it would be too great a burden on parties to a tax sale to require them to ascertain all who have a lien or claim an interest in the subject matter of the sale. Yet only two years later, in *Buncombe County v. Penland*, 206 N.C. 299, 173 S.E. 609 (1934), the court stated that it would be relatively easy, in a tax foreclosure action, to make all who have an interest in the land parties to the controversy. And again fifteen years later the court broadly stated that "all persons having an interest in

FORM **6.** RECORD OF FORECLOSURE SUIT

Record of Foreclosure Suit

Title of case: ____

| Taxpayer | Spouse | Address | Telephone |

Additional parties | Address | Telephone

| Tax Block   Lot   Twshp.   Street | Tax block   Lot   Twshp.   Street |

| Taxes due for each lot | Assessments (Prin.) (Int.)   (Tot.) |

| Total taxes | Total assessments |

Costs

Clerk of superior court   Attorney filing complaint

                                           Judgment

Sheriff _________________ Co.   First sale

Newspaper publisher   Second sale

Register of deeds

Total costs

Action	**Date**
Complaint filed	_______________________
Summonses delivered for service	_______________________

Record of Service of Summonses

Names of Defendants	Orig. Summons			Alias Summons		Pluries Summons	
	Iss'd	Srv'd	Endr'd	Iss'd	Srv'd	Iss'd	Srv'd

<table>
<tr><td align="center">Action</td><td align="center">Date</td></tr>
<tr><td>Publication (service of summonses)</td><td>1 _______________________</td></tr>
<tr><td></td><td>2 _______________________</td></tr>
<tr><td></td><td>3 _______________________</td></tr>
<tr><td>Judgment</td><td>_______________________</td></tr>
<tr><td>Notice of sale posted</td><td>_______________________</td></tr>
<tr><td>Publication</td><td>1 _______________________</td></tr>
<tr><td></td><td>2 _______________________</td></tr>
<tr><td></td><td>3 _______________________</td></tr>
<tr><td></td><td>4 _______________________</td></tr>
<tr><td>Sale</td><td>_______________________</td></tr>
<tr><td>Report of sale</td><td>_______________________</td></tr>
<tr><td>Resale</td><td>_______________________</td></tr>
<tr><td>Motion for confirmation</td><td>_______________________</td></tr>
<tr><td>Confirmation</td><td>_______________________</td></tr>
<tr><td>Deed delivered</td><td>_______________________</td></tr>
<tr><td>Final report</td><td>_______________________</td></tr>
<tr><td>Additional remarks</td><td></td></tr>
</table>

the equity of redemption should be parties to a proceeding for fore-closure."[4] The lesson of the more recent cases is that every reasonable effort should be made to ascertain and serve all interested parties.

In those cases in which the property is subject to the lien of a deed of trust, G.S. 105-374(c1) indicates that both the trustee and the beneficiary should be named as parties and served with process, and this appears to be consistent with case law from other states on this question.[5]

In foreclosing the lien on property in which there is a life estate, both the life tenant and the remainderman must be made parties and served with process.[6]

4. Wilmington v. Merrick, 231 N.C. 297, 299, 56 S.E. 643 (1949). *See also* Eason v. Spence, 232 N.C. 579, 61 S.E.2d 255 (1950).

5. See 55 Am. Jur. 2d *Mortages* § 647 (1996).

6. Board of Comm'rs v. Bumpass, 233 N.C. 190, 63 S.E.2d 144 (1951).

RECORD OF FORECLOSURE SUIT

Form 6 needs no explanation; essentially, it is a checklist to help ascertain that all necessary steps in bringing the action have been taken and a record of the dates when they were taken.

THE COMPLAINT

The filing of the complaint (Form 7) with the court commences the action (G.S. 1A-1, Rule 3). All pleadings subsequent to the complaint and all papers required to be served on a party must be filed with the clerk of court (G.S. 1A-1, Rule 5). Although the complaint is not required to be verified (G.S. 1A-1, Rule 11), many attorneys bringing foreclosure actions have the tax collector verify it so that a separate affidavit is not required when a default judgment is sought.

G.S. 105-374(c1) requires that each lienholder named in the caption of the complaint and other documents be designated "lienholder" after the name. This requirement applies to all lienholders, including trustees and beneficiaries in deeds of trust and judgment creditors.

The names of all parties must be set forth in the caption of the complaint, but G.S. 1A-1, Rule 10(a), permits the names of only the first party on each side, with an indication of additional parties—such as *et al.*— to be used in the captions of subsequent pleadings. The names of all parties should be set forth in the judgment.

G.S. 105-374(d) provides (1) that the complaint serves as a notice of action pending from the time it is filed with the clerk of superior court, and (2) that the complaint need not be cross-indexed as a notice of *lis pendens* to bind persons who may acquire an interest in the property after the complaint is filed. Therefore, the complaint need not be indexed in the Index to Judgments, Liens, and Lis Pendens.

According to *Board of Commissioners v. Bumpass*,[7] the body of the complaint should recite the names of the defendants and give their status (owner of the land, former owner, heirs of deceased owner, lienholders, etc.).

If much time has elapsed between the completion of the title search and the filing of the complaint, the attorney should update the search to see whether title to the property has been transferred and to discover any additional lienholders.

The foreclosure action must be instituted in the appropriate division of the General Court of Justice. If the total recovery sought is $10,000 or less, the district court is the proper division; if the amount is greater than $10,000, the superior court is the proper division.[8]

7. *Id.*

8. N.C. GEN. STAT. § 7A-243.

FORM 7. THE COMPLAINT

STATE OF NORTH CAROLINA

COUNTY OF _______________________

File # _________________________________

In the General Court of Justice

_______________________Court Division

____

Plaintiff

vs.

COMPLAINT

____

Defendant(s)

The plaintiff, complaining of the defendant(s), alleges:

1.   That plaintiff is a body politic and corporate of North Carolina and as such has power and authority to assess, levy, and collect taxes against real and personal property located within its boundaries in accordance with the laws of North Carolina.

2.   That defendant ____ is a resident of ____ County, North Carolina; that defendant ______________________________ is a resident of _______________________________; that the residence of defendant _________________________________ is unknown to plaintiff although plaintiff has made diligent inquiries in an effort to ascertain the address.

3.   That plaintiff is advised that the City [Town, County] of _____________________ may have or claim a lien for taxes and/or special assessments due it upon the real estate hereinafter described, and for that reason said defendant is made a party to this action.

4.   That the defendant _________________________, whose spouse is the defendant ______________________________, duly listed for taxes the real estate hereinafter described for the years _______, or the real estate was lawfully listed for taxation for those years on behalf of the defendant, and plaintiff lawfully assessed the real estate and levied taxes thereon for those years, which taxes remain unpaid as will hereinafter appear.

5.   That the records in the office of the Register of Deeds of ____________________ County reveal that the defendant _____________________, whose spouse is the defendant ______________________, owns the real estate hereinafter described as of the date this action was instituted.

6.   That there are due and owing to the plaintiff taxes which have been duly assessed and levied and that, by operation of Sections 105-355 and 105-356 of the General Statutes, constitute a first lien against the real estate hereinafter described.

That the amount of the lien including interest thereon as computed under the provisions of Section 105-360 of the General Statutes for each of the years indicated is set out below following the description of each tract, parcel, or lot to which the lien applies:

Form continues on next page. →

FORM 7. THE COMPLAINT (CONTINUED)

a.   Description: that tract, parcel, or lot of real estate situated in ___________________
Township, _______________________ County, North Carolina, and more particularly described
as follows:

[insert full legal description here].
[Tax map block and lot number may also be included.]

See deed from _______________ to _______________ recorded in the office of the Register of
Deeds of _____________________ County in Book _______, page ________.

Taxes:

Year	Amount (including interest)
_______	$_______________
_______	$_______________
Total taxes and interest due	$_______________

b.   Description: that tract, parcel, or lot of real estate situated in ___________________
Township, _______________________ County, North Carolina, and more particularly described
as follows:

[insert full legal description here].
[Tax map block and lot number may also be included.]

See deed from _______________ to _______________ recorded in the office of the Register of
Deeds of _____________________ County in Book ________, page _______.

Taxes:

Year	Amount (including interest)
_______	$_______________
_______	$_______________
Total taxes and interest due	$_______________

That all of such taxes remain due and owing to the plaintiff, although demand has been
made for the payment thereof;

That taxes for subsequent years may accrue or come due upon the property before the termination of this action; that such subsequently accruing taxes will also constitute a lien upon the
real estate; that plaintiff will present to the court the certificate of the tax collector for [insert name
of taxing unit] with respect to such taxes at the time judgment is prayed herein and will ask that
such subsequent taxes be included in the judgment.

7.   The interest of the defendant above-named other than the owner and spouse as disclosed by the public records of ________________ County, North Carolina, is set out in the appendix attached hereto and is hereby incorporated by reference and requested to be taken as part of this paragraph as if fully set out herein.

8.   In the event that payment of taxes is tendered before the judgment of sale is confirmed, defendants are given notice that before this action will be dismissed, the costs of this action must be paid, including attorney's fees, and that defendants have a right to a hearing before the court on the amount of attorney's fees.

Wherefore, plaintiff prays:

1.   That it have and recover a judgment against the owners of the property described in paragraph 5 of this complaint for the amount of taxes and interest due it as set out above plus any subsequently accruing taxes and penalties, interest, and costs thereon as allowed by law and the costs of this action; that said taxes, interest, and costs be declared a first lien upon the real estate described in paragraph 6 of this complaint.

2.   That a commissioner be appointed to sell the real estate described in paragraph 6 of this complaint, after due advertisement in accordance with law and under the direction of this court, and to deliver to the purchaser at such sale a deed to said real estate in fee simple, free and clear of all encumbrances, and that the interests and equities of redemption of the defendant in the property be forever barred and foreclosed.

3.   That the commissioner be ordered to pay from the proceeds of sale of the property the taxes, penalties, interests, and costs due the plaintiff, together with the costs of this action, and to pay the surplus, if any, to such parties as may be entitled thereto or pay it into court for the benefit of said parties.

4.   For such other and further relief as the court may deem just and proper.

____

Attorney for Plaintiff

____

Address

____

Telephone

Form continues on next page. →

FORM 7. THE COMPLAINT (CONTINUED)

State of North Carolina
County of ________________________________

________________________________, being duly sworn, deposes and says that he is the tax collector for the plaintiff taxing unit in the above-entitled action; that he has read the foregoing complaint and knows the contents thereof; and that the same is true of his own knowledge, except as to matters therein stated to be alleged on information and belief, and as to those matters he believes them to be true.

____
Tax Collector

Sworn to and subscribed before me this ________________________________ day of ________________________, __________.

Appendix

Deeds of Trust

1. Deed of trust executed by ________________________________ to ________________________, trustee for ________________________ recorded in Book ________, page ________, in the amount of $________________.

2. Deed of trust executed by ________________________________ to ________________________, trustee for ________________________, recorded in Book ________, page ______, in the amount of $________________.

Judgments

1. Judgment against ________________________, the defendant therein, in favor of ________________________, the plaintiff therein, in the amount of $______ plus interest and costs, recorded in Judgment Docket ________, page ______.

2. Judgment against ________________________, the defendant therein, in favor of ________________________, the plaintiff therein, in the amount of $______ plus interest and costs, recorded in Judgment Docket ________, page ______.

Other Liens and Interests

[Here set out any other liens, such as federal or state tax liens of record, materialmen's liens (including those not filed if the attorney has knowledge of them and the time for filing has not expired), contingent interests, etc.—in short, any interest that, if left outstanding, would constitute a defect in the title.]

THE SUMMONS

The requirements for the contents of the summons (Form 8) are set out in G.S. 1A-1, Rule 4(b):

> The summons shall run in the name of the State and be dated and signed by the clerk, assistant clerk, or deputy clerk of the court in the county in which the action is commenced. It shall contain the title of the cause and the name of the court and county wherein the action has been commenced. It shall be directed to the defendant or defendants and shall notify each defendant to appear and answer within 30 days after its service upon him and further that if he fails so to appear, the plaintiff will apply to the court for the relief demanded in the complaint. It shall set forth the name and address of plaintiff's attorney, or, if there be none, the name and address of plaintiff. If a request for admission is served with the summons, the summons shall so state.

G.S. 1A-1, Rule 4(c), states the time limitations within which the summons must be served:

> Personal service or substituted personal service of summons as prescribed by Rule 4(j)(1) a and b must be made within 60 days after the date of the issuance of summons. When a summons has been served upon every party named in the summons, it shall be returned immediately to the clerk who issued it, with notation thereon of its service.
>
> Failure to make service within the time allowed or failure to return a summons to the clerk after it has been served on every party named in the summons shall not invalidate the summons. If the summons is not served within the time allowed upon every party named in the summons, it shall be returned immediately upon the expiration of such time by the officer to the clerk of court who issued it with notation thereon of its nonservice and the reasons therefor as to every such party not served, but failure to comply with this requirement shall not invalidate the summons.

In computing the time during which the sheriff can make a valid service of summons and in which extensions of the period may be obtained, the term "issuance of summons" is important. The time within which service can be made and the time within which an alias summons or an endorsement of the original summons must be obtained are both measured from the date that the original summons was issued. G.S. 1A-1, Rule 4(a), provides that a "summons is issued when, after being filled out and dated, it is signed by the officer having authority to do so. The date the summons bears shall be prima facie evidence of the date of issue."

FORM 8. THE SUMMONS

STATE OF NORTH CAROLINA

File No.

_______________ County

In The General Court Of Justice
☐ District ☐ Superior Court Division

Name Of Plaintiff

Address

City, State, Zip

CIVIL SUMMONS

☐ **ALIAS AND PLURIES SUMMONS**

VERSUS

Name Of Defendant(s)

G.S. 1A-1, Rules 3, 4

Date Original Summons Issued

Date(s) Subsequent Summons(es) Issued

To Each Of The Defendant(s) Named Below:

Name And Address Of Defendant 1

Name And Address Of Defendant 2

A Civil Action Has Been Commenced Against You!

You are notified to appear and answer the complaint of the plaintiff as follows:

1. Serve a copy of your written answer to the complaint upon the plaintiff or plaintiff's attorney within thirty (30) days after you have been served. You may serve your answer by delivering a copy to the plaintiff or by mailing it to the plaintiff's last known address, and

2. File the original of the written answer with the Clerk of Superior Court of the county named above.

If you fail to answer the complaint, the plaintiff will apply to the Court for the relief demanded in the complaint.

Name And Address Of Plaintiff's Attorney (If None, Address Of Plaintiff)

Date Issued

Time ☐ AM ☐ PM

Signature

☐ Deputy CSC   ☐ Assistant CSC   ☐ Clerk Of Superior Court

☐ **ENDORSEMENT**
This Summons was originally issued on the date indicated above and returned not served. At the request of the plaintiff, the time within which this Summons must be served is extended sixty (60) days.

Date Of Endorsement

Time ☐ AM ☐ PM

Signature

☐ Deputy CSC   ☐ Assistant CSC   ☐ Clerk Of Superior Court

NOTE TO PARTIES: *Many counties have* **MANDATORY ARBITRATION** *programs in which most cases where the amount in controversy is $15,000 or less are heard by an arbitrator before a trial. The parties will be notified if this case is assigned for mandatory arbitration, and, if so, what procedure is to be followed.*

AOC-CV-100 Rev. 10/01
◊ 2001 Administrative Office of the Courts

(Over)

If a minor with an interest in the property sought to be foreclosed has a general guardian, both the minor and the general guardian or parent must be served with a summons and a copy of the complaint. If the minor has no parent or general guardian and there is no other person having custody or control of the minor, a guardian *ad litem* must be appointed to represent his or her interest in the foreclosure action. But before a guardian *ad litem* can be appointed, service must be made upon the minor, who alone should be named in the summons, because the court has no jurisdiction over the defendant until the defendant is prop-

RETURN OF SERVICE

I certify that this Summons and a copy of the complaint were received and served as follows:

DEFENDANT 1

Date Served	Time Served	Name Of Defendant
	☐ AM ☐ PM	

☐ By delivering to the defendant named above a copy of the summons and complaint.

☐ By leaving a copy of the summons and complaint at the dwelling house or usual place of abode of the defendant named above with a person of suitable age and discretion then residing therein.

☐ As the defendant is a corporation, service was effected by delivering a copy of the summons and complaint to the person named below.

Name And Address Of Person With Whom Copies Left (If corporation, give title of person copies left with)

☐ Other manner of service (specify)

☐ Defendant WAS NOT served for the following reason:

DEFENDANT 2

Date Served	Time Served	Name Of Defendant
	☐ AM ☐ PM	

☐ By delivering to the defendant named above a copy of the summons and complaint.

☐ By leaving a copy of the summons and complaint at the dwelling house or usual place of abode of the defendant named above with a person of suitable age and discretion then residing therein.

☐ As the defendant is a corporation, service was effected by delivering a copy of the summons and complaint to the person named below.

Name And Address Of Person With Whom Copies Left (If corporation, give title of person copies left with)

☐ Other manner of service (specify)

☐ Defendant WAS NOT served for the following reason.

Service Fee Paid	Signature Of Deputy Sheriff Making Return
$	
Date Received	Name Of Sheriff (Type Or Print)
Date Of Return	County Of Sheriff

AOC-CV-100 Side Two. Rev. 10/01
© 2001 Administrative Office of the Courts

erly served, and thus no authority to appoint the guardian *ad litem* until the minor is served.[9] On the other hand, G.S. 1A-1, Rule 17(c)(3), expressly states that if service is made by publication upon minors or incompetents, a guardian *ad litem* may be appointed before publication is complete, and the guardian shall be served with a copy of the complaint. While in the first instance failure to serve the minor before the

9. Hughes v. Pritchard, 153 N.C. 135, 69 S.E. 3 (1910); *see also* N.C. Gen. Stat. § 1A-1, Rules 4(j)(2) and 17(c)(2).

guardian *ad litem* is appointed renders the proceeding irregular, the proceeding is not void, and it may be cured by subsequent service on the minor and the filing of an answer by the guardian *ad litem*.[10]

Better results will be obtained if the defendants' addresses, when known, are shown on the summons or if information—such as their employers, last known addresses, etc.—is given to the sheriff to help him locate the parties. The plaintiff's attorney is responsible for seeing that the summonses are delivered to the proper officer for service.

Great care should be used in checking returns on the summons. The names should appear in the return exactly as shown on the summons. If service is made on a corporate defendant or governmental unit, the attorney should see that it is made on a proper officer. [See G.S. 1A-1, Rule 4(j)(3), (4), (5), (6), (7), and (8) for the proper officers to accept service of process.]

ADDITIONAL TIME FOR SERVICE

Often the sheriff or other officer to whom the summons is delivered for service is unable to serve it on every defendant named therein within the time provided by statute. Under such circumstances the time in which the summons can be served may be extended. Pursuant to G.S. 1A-1, Rule 4(d), either the clerk may endorse the original summons, or a new summons —an alias and pluries summons—may be issued. Form 8 is set up for either method of extending the time for service.

G.S. 1A-1, Rule 4(d), provides: "in tax and assessment foreclosures under . . . G.S. 105-374, the first endorsement may be made at any time within two years after the issuance of the original summons, and subsequent endorsements may thereafter be made as in other actions; or an alias or pluries summons may be sued out at any time within two years after the issuance of the original summons, and after the issuance of such alias or pluries summons, the chain of summonses may be kept up as in any other action." Thus the period within which the first extension of time for service of summons can be obtained is longer for tax proceedings than for ordinary civil proceedings. But the period within which to obtain subsequent extensions in tax proceedings is expressly declared to be the same as in other civil proceedings. This period is within ninety days of the issuance of the prior summons or the last endorsement on the original summons.

The effect of failure to keep the chain of summonses alive in the above manner is stated in G.S. 1A-1, Rule 4(e):

10. Dudley v. Tyson, 167 N.C. 67, 82 S.E. 1025 (1914).

When there is neither endorsement by the clerk nor issuance of alias or pluries summons within the time specified in Rule 4(d), the action is discontinued as to any defendant not theretofore served with summons within the time allowed. Thereafter, alias or pluries summons may issue, or an extension be endorsed by the clerk, but, as to such defendant, the action shall be deemed to have commenced on the date of such issuance or endorsement.

This statute means that if an alias or pluries summons is issued or the original summons is endorsed after the time specified in Rule 4(d), the summons no longer serves as a continuance of the original action but operates as the beginning of a new action. The running of the ten-year statute of limitations applicable to tax actions will therefore be measured to the time when the new action begins rather than to the time the complaint was filed, as it would have been if the renewal summonses or endorsements had been obtained within the time provided by the statute.

PROOF OF SERVICE

Many of the judgments obtained in foreclosure actions are by default. G.S. 1A-1, Rule 4(j2), requires that before a default judgment may be made, proof of service of process must be made, and the nature of the proof required depends on the type of service used. Rule 4(j2)(1), by reference to G.S. 1-75.10(1), provides that if service is by personal delivery by a North Carolina sheriff or other process server, the serving officer's certificate is sufficient proof of service.[11] If service is by registered or certified mail, Rule 4(j2)(2), by reference to G.S. 1-75.10(4), requires proof by an affidavit of mailing. Form 9 is for this affidavit. If service is by a designated delivery service [see G.S. 1A-1, Rule 4(j)(1)(d)], Rule 4(j2)(2), by reference to G.S. 1-75.10(5), requires an affidavit regarding deposit with the designated delivery service. Form 10 is for this affidavit. In the case of service by publication, Rule 4(j2)(3) requires proof by three affidavits, and the forms for these affidavits—Forms 14, 15, and 16—follow the discussion of service by publication.

SERVICE OUTSIDE THE STATE

Process on parties outside North Carolina is served by the same methods used for in-state parties: personal delivery, registered or certified mail, designated delivery service, or publication. If the out-of-state party's address is known to the attorney bringing the foreclosure, service by mail

---

11. The completed return of the summons serves as the proof required by this statute. *See* Williams v. Burroughs Wellcome Co., 46 N.C. App. 459, 265 S.E.2d 633 (1980).

FORM 9. PROOF OF SERVICE BY REGISTERED OR CERTIFIED MAIL

STATE OF NORTH CAROLINA   File # _______________________________

COUNTY OF _____________________   In the General Court of Justice
                                           _____________________ Court Division

____
Plaintiff

vs.   AFFIDAVIT

____
Defendant(s)

____ , being sworn, says:

That he or she is attorney for the plaintiff in the above-styled action now pending in this court; that the action is to foreclose the lien of taxes due the plaintiff upon certain real estate described in the complaint filed in the action; that _____________________ is a defendant in the action; that a copy of the summons and complaint addressed to the defendant was deposited in a United States Post Office for mailing by registered [certified] mail, return receipt requested, on _____________________, _______; that the mailed copies of the summons and complaint were in fact received by the defendant on _____________________, _______, as evidenced by the attached registry receipt (or other acceptable evidence of delivery); and that the genuine receipt showing delivery of the summons and complaint upon the defendant (or other evidence of delivery) is attached to this affidavit. This affidavit is made pursuant to Section 1A-1, Rule 4(j2)(2), prerequisite to a prayer for judgment by default against the defendant named herein.

____
                                           Attorney for Plaintiff

____
                                           Address

____
                                           Telephone

Sworn to and subscribed before me, this _______ day of _____________________, _______.

____
(Signature of officer authorized
to administer oaths)

FORM 10. PROOF OF SERVICE BY A DESIGNATED DELIVERY SERVICE

STATE OF NORTH CAROLINA   File # ________________________________

COUNTY OF _______________________   In the General Court of Justice
                                         ____________________ Court Division

____
Plaintiff

vs.   AFFIDAVIT

____
Defendant(s)

____, being sworn, says:

That he or she is attorney for the plaintiff in the above-styled action now pending in this court; that the action is to foreclose the lien of taxes due the plaintiff upon certain real estate described in the complaint filed in the action; that _____________________ is a defendant in the action; that a copy of the summons and complaint addressed to the defendant was deposited with _________________, a designated delivery service as authorized under G.S. 1A-1, Rule 4, delivery receipt requested, on ______________, _____; that it was in fact received as evidenced by the attached delivery receipt (or other evidence of delivery to the addressee _______________); that the genuine receipt or other evidence of delivery is attached. This affidavit is made pursuant to Section 1A-1, Rule 4(j2)(2), prerequisite to a prayer for judgment by default against the defendant named herein.

                                ____
                                               Attorney for Plaintiff
                                ____
                                                         Address
                                ____
                                                       Telephone

Sworn to and subscribed before me, this _____ day of _________________, _______.

____
(Signature of officer authorized
 to administer oaths)

FORM 11. LETTER OF INSTRUCTIONS TO SHERIFF
OR OTHER OFFICER SERVING THE SUMMONS

Dear _________________________________:

As attorney for the County [City or Town] of _________________________, North Carolina, I am enclosing herewith an original summons issued in a case pending in the _________________________ Court for _________________________ County against the defendants named therein, together with a copy of the summons, which is attached to a copy of the complaint filed in the action for each defendant. I ask that you serve the summons by leaving with each defendant a copy of the summons and complaint. I am told that the defendants may be found at the addresses shown on the summons.

After serving defendants, please fill in the enclosed affidavit of service; then take it to the clerk of your court of general jurisdiction or other official authorized to administer oaths and have him or her administer the oath and affix his or her official seal as indicated. The form is drawn in accordance with our statute and must be filled out exactly as drawn in order to be effective. Please return the form and the original summons, with the return completed, to me in the enclosed self-addressed envelope as soon as you have effected service and completed the affidavit. If any of the defendants on whom service was made are minors or are insane or otherwise incompetent, please indicate this fact on the summons. If any of the defendants cannot be found in your county, please state this fact on the summons and advise me where these defendants can be found.

If you will tell me your fee for serving this process and the clerk's fee for administering the oath, I will send you a check immediately.

Very truly yours,

____

Attorney for [City]

[County] of _________________________________

is obviously much less expensive than the other methods of service. If the address is not known or if personal service is thought preferable for any other reason, G.S. 1A-1, Rule 4(a), provides that out-of-state service may be made by any person twenty-one years old or older and not a party to the suit, or by any person authorized to serve summons by the law of the place where the service is to be made.

Form 11 is a letter of explanation to accompany the process to be served by an out-of-state officer. Because G.S. 1-75.10(1)(b) details the requirements of the affidavit of service made by the officer serving process outside the state, and because this form may differ from that which the officer is accustomed to executing, a letter of instructions to the officer to whom the summons is directed may help secure compliance with the statutory requirements.

FORM 12. PROOF OF SERVICE BY OUT-OF-STATE OFFICER
[AFFIDAVIT FOR PROOF OF SERVICE, G.S. 1-75.10(1)B]

STATE OF NORTH CAROLINA   File # ________________________________

COUNTY OF _____________________   ______________In the General Court of Justice

                                           _______________________________ Court Division

____

Plaintiff

vs.   AFFIDAVIT OF SERVICE

____

Defendant(s)

I, ____, being sworn, do certify that I am an
official qualified to make service of process in the State of _______________________________
by virtue of authority contained in [here cite statutory authority] and by virtue of my office as
____; that on the ________ day of
_______________________, ______, at _______________________ Street, City of
_______________________, ____ County,
_________________State of _______________________________, I delivered a copy
of the summons and attached complaint in the above-entitled action to _________________________,
defendant, knowing him or her to be the party mentioned in the summons, and left with him or
her a copy of the summons and complaint [or if defendant was not personally served, state where
and with whom copy was left]. This affidavit is made pursuant to Section 1-75.10(1)b of the
General Statutes of North Carolina relative to service of process outside of North Carolina.

                                           ____

                                           Name and title of affiant

Sworn to and subscribed before me, this ________ day of _______________________, ______.

____

(Signature of officer authorized
to administer oaths)

Form 12 is a proof-of-service affidavit to be completed by the officer in order to satisfy the requirements of G.S. 1A-1, Rule 4(j2)(1), if a default judgment is sought.

SERVICE BY PUBLICATION

G.S. 1A-1, Rule 4(j1), provides that a party "that cannot with due diligence be served by personal delivery, registered or certified mail, or by a designated delivery service may be served by publication."

FORM 13. NOTICE OF SERVICE OF PROCESS BY PUBLICATION

STATE OF NORTH CAROLINA

COUNTY OF ___________________

File # ___________________________

In the General Court of Justice

___________________________ Court Division

____

Plaintiff

vs.

NOTICE OF SERVICE

OF PROCESS BY PUBLICATION

____

Defendant(s)

To ___________________ :

Take notice that a pleading seeking relief against you has been filed in the above-entitled action.

The nature of the relief being sought is as follows: foreclosure sale to satisfy unpaid property taxes on your interest in the property described as lot _______, block _______, which is more completely described in the complaint. Plaintiff seeks to extinguish any and all claim or interest that you may have in the property.

You are required to make defense to such pleading not later than ___________________, and upon your failure to do so, the party seeking service against you will apply to the court for the relief sought.

This __________ day of ___________________, ______.

____

Attorney for Plaintiff

____

Address

____

Telephone

Also, G.S. 105-374(c) provides that "Persons who have disappeared or who cannot be located and persons whose names and whereabouts are unknown, and all possible heirs or assignees of such persons may be served by publication; and such persons, their heirs, and assignees may be designated by general description or by fictitious names in such an action."

Service by publication consists of publishing a notice of service of process for three successive weeks in a newspaper qualified for legal advertising in accordance with G.S. 1-597. Pursuant to G.S. 1A-1, Rule 4(k)(1), publication is required to be made only in the county in which the action is pending.

If the post office address of the party being served by publication is known or can be ascertained with due diligence, then a copy of the notice must be mailed to the party at or before the time of the first publication.

Under any authority to use service by publication, "due diligence" must actually have been exercised to ascertain that the persons concerned cannot be served personally or by mail. A recitation to that effect in the return or in the required affidavits, if in fact due diligence has not been exercised, is not enough.[12]

Rule 4(j1) specifies that the notice of service of process by publication shall

1. designate the court in which the action has been commenced and the title of the action;
2. be directed to the defendant sought to be served;
3. state that a pleading seeking relief against the person to be served has been filed, has been required to be filed, or has been required to be filed therein not later than a date specified in the notice;
4. state the nature of the relief being sought;
5. require the defendant being served to make defense to the pleading within forty days after a date stated in the notice, exclusive of such date, which date so stated shall be the date of the first publication of notice, or the date when the complaint is required to be filed, whichever is later, and notify the defendant that upon his failure to do so the party seeking service of process by publication will apply to the court for the relief sought;
6. be subscribed by the party seeking service or his attorney and give the post office address of the party or his attorney.

Form 13 fulfills the requirements of Rule (j1) and is for use as the notice of publication.

PROOF OF SERVICE BY PUBLICATION

When service of process is by publication, the statutes impose several overlapping requirements for affidavits proving that service. G.S. 1A-1, Rule 4(j1), requires that when the publication is completed, "there shall be filed with the court an affidavit showing the publication and mailing in accordance with the requirements of G.S. 1-75.10(2), the circumstances warranting the use of service by publication, and information, if

12. *See* Wilmington v. Merrick, 231 N.C. 297, 56 S.E.2d 643 (1949); Galer v. Auburn-Asheville Co., 204 N.C. 683, 169 S.E. 642 (1933); and *In re* Phillips, 18 N.C. App. 65, 196 S.E.2d 59 (1973).

FORM 14. AFFIDAVIT OF SERVICE BY PUBLICATION

STATE OF NORTH CAROLINA

COUNTY OF ______________________

File # _______________________________

In the General Court of Justice

_______________________________ Court Division

____

Plaintiff

vs.

AFFIDAVIT OF SERVICE
BY PUBLICATION

____

Defendant(s)

______________________, being sworn, says:

That the affiant is attorney for the plaintiff in the above-entitled action;

That ______________________________ is a defendant in the above-entitled action;

That a cause of action exists against the above-named defendant in which process may be served by publication as provided by G.S. 1A-1, Rule 4(j), as the subject of the action is real property in ______________________ County, North Carolina, and the defendant has or claims an interest in the real property, and the relief demanded consists wholly or partially in excluding the defendant from any interest therein, as provided by G.S. 1-175.8;

That after the exercise of due diligence the plaintiff was unable to serve the above-named defendant by delivering a copy of the summons and complaint to the defendant personally either within or without the state of North Carolina or by leaving a copy of the summons and complaint at the place of abode of defendant with some person of suitable age and discretion residing therein;

That plaintiff after the exercise of due diligence was unable to ascertain the usual place of abode, residence, post office box or other address, or the whereabouts of the above-named defendant and was therefore unable to serve him or her with a copy of the summons and complaint by registered or certified mail;

That after the exercise of due diligence plaintiff was unable to obtain any information concerning the present location of the above-named defendant, or that, according to information available to plaintiff, the last known location of the defendant was [city and state indicated by available information], and therefore the notice was published in a newspaper circulated in that city;

That pursuant to G.S. 1A-1, Rule 4(j1), service of process by publication was commenced as to the defendant on _______________________________, _______, in [name of newspaper], City of _______________________________, _______________________ County, [name of state], and completed on _______________________, _______.

____

Attorney for the Plaintiff

____

Address

____

Telephone

Sworn to and subscribed before me, this _______ day of ________________, _______.

____

(Signature of officer authorized to administer oaths)

FORM 15. PUBLISHER'S AFFIDAVIT

STATE OF NORTH CAROLINA

COUNTY OF ___________________

File # ______________________________

In the General Court of Justice

______________________ Court Division

____

Plaintiff

vs.   AFFIDAVIT

____

Defendant(s)

___________________, being sworn, says:

That he or she is the ___________________* of the ___________________ Company engaged in publishing a newspaper known as _______________________________, published, issued, and entered as second-class mail in the City of ___________________, in said county and state;

That he or she is authorized to make this affidavit and sworn statement;

That the notice, a true copy of which is attached hereto, was first published in said newspaper on ___________________ and on ___________________, and last published on ___________________; and that the newspaper in which such notice was published was, at the time of each and every such publication, a newspaper meeting all the requirements and qualifications of Section 1-597 of the General Statutes.

This ___________ day of ___________________, ________.

____

Affiant

____

Notary Public

My commission expires ___________________, ________.

Sworn to and subscribed before me, this _______ day of ___________________, ________.

*Insert here the proper designation of affiant's position with the newspaper, such as owner, publisher, editor, managing editor, or business manager. (See G.S. 1-600 for a list of the officials authorized to make affidavit of publication.)

any, regarding the location of the party served." G.S. 1-75.10(2), in turn, requires two affidavits—one from the printer or publisher showing the notice and giving the dates of the first and last publication, and one certifying the mailing of the notice by the person who mailed it. Rule 4(j2)(3) requires that an affidavit of publication be filed before a default

FORM 16. MAILING NOTICE OF SERVICE BY PUBLICATION

STATE OF NORTH CAROLINA

COUNTY OF _______________________

File # _________________________________

In the General Court of Justice

_________________________ Court Division

____

Plaintiff

vs.

AFFIDAVIT OF MAILING

OF NOTICE OF SERVICE

OF PROCESS BY PUBLICATION

____

Defendant(s)

_____________________________________, being sworn, says:

That in the above-entitled action he or she is attorney for the plaintiff;

That _________________________________, defendant in the above-mentioned action, has been served with process by means of publication pursuant to G.S. 1A-1, Rule 4(j1), such publication having been commenced on _________________________________, _________, and completed on _________________________, _________;

That a copy of the notice of service of process by publication was mailed to the defendant at _________________________________, on _________________________________, _________; (or)

That the defendant's address could not be ascertained after the exercise of due diligence and therefore no copy of the notice of service of process by publication was mailed to him or her.

____

Attorney for the Plaintiff

____

Address

____

Telephone

Sworn to and subscribed before me, this _______________ day of _________________________, _______.

____

(Signature of officer authorized
to administer oaths)

judgment may be obtained, and that this affidavit show "the circumstances warranting the use of service by publication, information, if any, regarding the location of the party served which was used in determining the area in which service by publication was printed and proof of service in accordance with G.S. 1-75.10(2)."

The elements of the general affidavit required by G.S. 1A-1, Rule 4(j1), and the affidavit required by Rule 4(j2)(3) can be combined in one affidavit, and Form 14 is for that affidavit. Form 15 is for the publisher's affidavit, and Form 16 is for the affidavit of mailing, if the notice is mailed. When service by publication is on unknown defendants, Form 17 should be used rather than Form 14.

SERVICE BY PUBLICATION
ON UNKNOWN PERSONS

Unknown defendants—such as possible heirs whose names and whereabouts cannot be learned—constitute a major problem for the taxing unit's attorney in bringing a foreclosure action. As noted above, G.S. 105-374(c) authorizes service by publication on unknown persons, their heirs, and assignees. Additional authority for the use of service by publication on unknown defendants is in G.S. 1A-1, Rule 4(k)(2), which states that in actions in which the jurisdiction is *in rem* or *quasi in rem*, "If the defendant is unknown, he may be designated by description and process may be served by publication in the manner provided in section (j1)." The notice is required to be published only in the county where the action is pending.

Although *Wilmington v. Merrick*, 231 N.C. 297, 56 S.E.2d 643 (1949), was decided under the predecessors of G.S. 105-374(c), it is still relevant. This case says that if the defendants in a foreclosure are "Heirs of John Doe," if service is by publication, and if before sale of the property some of the heirs are identified, then the plaintiff taxing unit must apply for an order naming those heirs as defendants and should serve them with process.

Note that if a party is unknown (or if it is not known whether the party is living or dead), it will also be impossible to know whether he or she is a minor or otherwise incompetent or is a member of the armed forces. Thus guardians *ad litem* should be appointed for such unknown parties as may be minors or incompetents, and, pursuant to the Soldiers' and Sailors' Civil Relief Act, 50 U.S.C. App. § 520, attorneys should be appointed for defendants who may be in the armed services.

In Form 17, an effort has been made—by way of illustration—to set up a style or title for a foreclosure action that will cover all unknown parties and all lienors and persons claiming under the unknown parties. The names in the form are not intended to be "fictitious names." John Davis is the name of the "last listing taxpayer." If the name of the last taxpayer is not available, the attorney will have to use either a fictitious name for the last listing taxpayer or a general description of him.

FORM 17. **AFFIDAVIT OF SERVICE BY PUBLICATION
ON UNKNOWN PERSONS**

STATE OF NORTH CAROLINA   File # ___________________________
COUNTY OF ___________________   In the General Court of Justice

                                                 _______________________ Court Division

____

Plaintiff   AFFIDAVIT OF SERVICE
vs.   BY PUBLICATION

JOHN DAVIS and MRS. JOHN DAVIS; all
assignees, heirs at law, and devisees of JOHN
DAVIS, if deceased, and of MRS. JOHN DAVIS, if
deceased, together with all their creditors and
lienholders regardless of how or through whom
they claim, and any and all persons claiming
any interest in the estate of JOHN DAVIS and the
estate of MRS. JOHN DAVIS, if deceased.

____

Defendant(s)

_______________________________, being sworn, says:

    That in the above-entitled action, he or she is the attorney for the plaintiff;

    That according to the information and belief of the affiant the above-named defendants are unknown to the plaintiff; that there appears on record in the Office of the Register of Deeds for _______________________________ County, in Book _____, page _____, a deed executed by William Brown to the defendant John Davis, dated May 5, 1927, conveying the real estate described in the complaint; that under date of June 6, 1932, the defendant John Davis and wife conveyed a one-half undivided interest in the property to Richard Rogers by deed recorded in the Office of the Register of Deeds for _______________________________ County, in Book _____, page _____; that the affiant has been unable to discover any deed of record conveying the other one-half undivided interest in this property, nor is there any record of the administration of the estate of said John Davis in the Office of the Clerk of the Superior Court for _________________ County; that affiant has made a diligent search in an effort to discover the whereabouts of John Davis and to discover whether John Davis and wife are living or dead; that affiant has visited the premises described in the complaint and has made inquiries there and in the neighborhood and has made other inquiries but has been unable to discover where John Davis and wife are and whether they are living or dead;

That a cause of action exists against the above-named defendants in which service of process may be made by publication as provided by G.S. 1A-1, Rule 4(j), as the subject of the action is real property in _______________________ County, North Carolina, and the defendants have or claim an interest in this real property, and the relief demanded consists wholly or partially in excluding the defendants from any interest therein, as provided by G.S. 1-75.8;

That after the exercise of due diligence the plaintiff was unable to serve the above-named defendants by delivering a copy of the summons and complaint to the defendants personally either within or without the State of North Carolina or by leaving a copy of the summons and complaint at the place of abode of defendants with some person of suitable age and discretion residing therein;

That plaintiff after exercise of due diligence was unable to ascertain the usual place of abode, residence, post office box or other address, or the whereabouts of the above-named defendants, and was therefore unable to serve them with a copy of the summons and complaint by registered or certified mail;

That pursuant to G.S. 1A-1, Rule 4(j1), service of process by publication was commenced as to the defendants on _______________________, _______, in [name of newspaper], City of _______________________, _______________________ County, North Carolina, and completed on _______________________, _______.

____

Attorney for the Plaintiff

____

Address

____

Telephone

Sworn to and subscribed before me, this _____ day of _______________________, _______.

____

(Signature of officer authorized
to administer oaths)

By way of illustration, the form recites the affiant's efforts to find the parties; it is useful to have such a recitation in the affidavit and in the foreclosure file.

MOTION FOR APPOINTMENT OF A GUARDIAN *AD LITEM*

G.S. 1A-1, Rule 17(b)(2), provides that infants and other incompetents (whether residents or nonresidents) must defend by their general or testamentary guardian if they have one within North Carolina. If they do not, and if "any of them have been summoned, the court in which said action . . . is pending, upon motion of any of the parties, may appoint some discreet person to act as guardian *ad litem*, to defend in behalf of" such individuals.

If an infant or other incompetent has no general guardian or guardian *ad litem* when the action is commenced, service of process can be had only on the infant or incompetent; if there is a guardian at the time the action is commenced, service should be made on both the infant or incompetent and the guardian. When a guardian *ad litem* is appointed, he should be served in the same manner as a party [G.S. 1A-1, Rule 4(j)(2)].

The consent of the person who is to serve as guardian (usually a lawyer) should be obtained before the motion is made, so that his or her name can appear in the motion and it can be stated that consent has been given.

The supreme court has held that a failure to serve an infant before the guardian *ad litem* is appointed renders the proceeding irregular but not void, and the irregularity may be cured by subsequent service on both infant and guardian and by the guardian's filing of an answer.[13]

The application should show the disability of the party, the nature of the action, the interest of the infant or incompetent, the absence of a guardian in the state, and proof that the infant or incompetent has been served with summons. Form 18 is drawn with these points in mind. Form 19 is for the supporting affidavit to accompany the motion.[14]

---

13. Dudley v. Tyson, 167 N.C. 67, 82 S.E. 1025 (1914).

14. N.C. GEN. STAT. § 1A-1, Rule 43(e), states: "When a motion is based on facts not appearing of record the court may hear the matter on affidavits presented by the respective parties, but the court may direct that the matter be heard wholly or partly on oral testimony or depositions."

ORDER OF APPOINTMENT
OF GUARDIAN *AD LITEM*

On finding that the disability exists, that the appointment is necessary, that a summons has been served, and that the person to be appointed is suitable to represent the infant or incompetent, the court should set out these findings in the order (Form 20) and make the appointment. After naming the guardian *ad litem*, the order should direct him or her to answer and defend the rights of the infant or incompetent defendant. The person so appointed may accept the appointment in writing (as provided at the bottom of the form below) or by proceeding to act in his or her capacity as guardian.

When appointed, the guardian *ad litem* should be served with both a summons and a copy of the complaint. G.S.1A-1, Rule 17, contemplates that in civil actions the guardian *ad litem* will actually file an answer. If the guardian *ad litem* fails to file an answer as required, he or she should be removed and another appointed.

In most cases the guardian *ad litem* is justified in admitting the allegations of the complaint. (They are based on matters of record and can be checked.) The guardian should not, however, act as a mere rubber stamp. If the guardian should file a mimeographed or printed form answer or merely sign an answer prepared by the plaintiff's attorney, he or she would not only create a bad impression but also lay the proceeding open to later attack. The guardian should make a reasonable investigation on his or her own account and should assert any defense discovered.

Neither the guardian *ad litem* nor the guardian's attorney should be connected with the plaintiff, even if the interest is only "colorable." The guardian's fee should be commensurate with the task to be performed —diligent protection of the interests of defendant infants and incompetents. This fee is to be taxed as part of the costs.[15]

DEFENDANT IN MILITARY SERVICE

Before a default judgment may be entered against a nonappearing defendant, 50 U.S.C. App. § 520 requires the plaintiff to file an affidavit stating that the defendant is not in the military service. If the plaintiff cannot file such an affidavit, then he must file an affidavit stating either that the defendant is in military service or that the plaintiff is unable to determine whether the defendant is is in military service and must request the appointment of an attorney to represent the nonappearing defendant

---

15. N.C. Gen. Stat. § 7A-305(d)(7); *id.* § 105-374(i).

FORM 18. MOTION FOR APPOINTMENT OF GUARDIAN *AD LITEM*

STATE OF NORTH CAROLINA

COUNTY OF ___________________________

File # _______________________________

In the General Court of Justice

_______________________ Court Division

Plaintiff

vs.

Defendant(s)

MOTION FOR APPOINTMENT

OF GUARDIAN *AD LITEM*

Now comes _______________________________, attorney for the plaintiff in the above-entitled action, and makes known to the court that _______________________________, defendant in the action for the foreclosure of a lien for taxes against real estate, is an infant [incompetent] and without a general or testamentary guardian in North Carolina, as shown in the affidavit annexed hereto as Exhibit A, and that the infant [incompetent] defendant has been duly served with summons in this action.

Wherefore, motion is hereby made to the court pursuant to Rule 17(c) of the Rules of Civil Procedure to appoint _______________________________, a suitable and discreet person, guardian *ad litem* for the infant [incompetent] defendant to represent the infant [incompetent] defendant's interest in this action.

This ___________ day of _____________________, _______.

____

Attorney for Plaintiff

____

Address

____

Telephone

before a default judgment may be entered. Form 21 is for the affidavit concerning military service, and Form 22 is for the motion for appointment of an attorney. Form 23 is for the order of appointment.

SERVICE ON THE UNITED STATES

If the title examination disclosed a federal tax or other sort of federal lien on the property being foreclosed, the United States will have been made a party defendant and designated a lienholder. In actions to foreclose a lien against property which also has a federal lien, 28 U.S.C. § 2410 requires that service shall be made on the United States by serving the United States attorney for the district in which the action is brought with copies

FORM 19. AFFIDAVIT IN SUPPORT OF MOTION
FOR APPOINTMENT OF GUARDIAN *AD LITEM*

STATE OF NORTH CAROLINA

COUNTY OF _______________________

File # _____________________________

In the General Court of Justice

_____________________ Court Division

____

Plaintiff

vs.

AFFIDAVIT

____

Defendant(s)

_______________________________, attorney for the plaintiff in the above-entitled action, being sworn, says that:

1.   [Name of defendant for whom appointment of guardian is sought] is a defendant in the above-entitled action and has been served with process by publication pursuant to G.S. 1A-1, Rule 4(j1);

2.   Affiant is unable to determine whether defendant is an infant or incompetent but believes that he or she may be; and

3.   To the best of affiant's knowledge and belief the defendant is without general or testamentary guardians.

OR

1.   [Name of defendant for whom appointment of guardian is sought] is a defendant in the above-entitled action, and the sheriff's return of service serving him or her with summons and other information available to the affiant indicates that he or she is an infant [incompetent]; and

2. To the best of affiant's knowledge and belief, the defendant is without general or testamentary guardians.

OR

1.   [Name of defendant for whom appointment of guardian is sought] is a defendant in the above-entitled action, and from the best information available to him or her affiant believes the defendant to be an infant [incompetent];

2.   To the best of affiant's knowledge and belief the defendant is without general or testamentary guardians.

____

Attorney for the Plaintiff

Sworn to and subscribed before me, this _______ day of _________________, _______.

____

(Signature of officer authorized
to administer oaths)

FORM 20. ORDER OF APPOINTMENT OF GUARDIAN *AD LITEM*

STATE OF NORTH CAROLINA

COUNTY OF _____________________

File # _________________________________

In the General Court of Justice

_____________________________ Court Division

____

Plaintiff

vs.

ORDER APPOINTING

GUARDIAN *AD LITEM*

____

Defendant(s)

_____________________________, attorney for the plaintiff in the above-entitled action, having moved for appointment of a guardian *ad litem* to represent _____________________________, defendant in this action, and it appearing to the court from [evidence received of disability] that defendant is an infant [incompetent] and is entitled to the appointment of a guardian *ad litem* and is without a general or testamentary guardian in North Carolina, and that the infant [incompetent] defendant has been duly served with summons in this action, and that _____________________________, who is found by the court, after due inquiry as to his or her fitness, to be a suitable, discreet, and competent person, has come into court and signified his or her willingness to accept the office of guardian *ad litem* and to represent the infant [incompetent];

It is, therefore, ordered that _____________________________ be appointed guardian *ad litem* for _____________________________ infant [incompetent] defendant in this action, and be directed to appear and defend the defendant in his or her behalf as guardian *ad litem*.

This _________ day of _____________________________, _______.

____

Clerk of Superior Court

_____________________________ County

Appointment accepted.

____

Guardian *ad litem*

____

of the summons and complaint and also by sending copies to the Attorney General in Washington, D.C., by registered or certified mail:

> The complaint or pleading shall set forth with particularity the nature of the interest or lien of the United States. In actions or suits involving liens arising under the internal revenue laws, the complaint or pleading shall include the name and address of the taxpayer whose liability created the lien and, if a notice of the tax lien was filed, the identity of the internal revenue office which filed the notice, and the date and place such notice of lien was filed. In actions in the State

FORM 21. AFFIDAVIT REGARDING WHETHER A DEFENDANT IS IN MILITARY SERVICE

STATE OF NORTH CAROLINA

COUNTY OF _____________________

File # _________________________________

In the General Court of Justice

_____________________________ Court Division

____

Plaintiff

vs.

AFFIDAVIT

____

Defendant(s)

_______________________________, attorney for the plaintiff in the above-entitled action, being sworn, says that:

1. [Name of defendant against whom default judgment is sought] is a defendant in the above-entitled action and has been served with process pursuant to G.S. 1A-1, Rule 4(j) [appropriate subsection number under which service was made];

2. To the best of affiant's knowledge and belief, the defendant is not as of the date of this action in military service.

OR

1. [Name of defendant against whom default judgment is sought] is a defendant in the above-entitled action and has been served with process by publication pursuant to G.S. 1A-1, Rule 4(1);

2. Affiant is unable to determine whether defendant is in military service;

3. This affidavit is made pursuant to the requirements of 50 U.S.C. App. § 520.

____

Attorney for the Plaintiff

Sworn to and subscribed before me this _________ day of ____________________, _______.

____

(Signature of officer authorized to administer oaths)

courts service upon the United States shall be made by serving the process of the court with a copy of the complaint upon the United States attorney for the district in which the action is brought or upon an assistant United States attorney or clerical employee designated by the United States attorney in writing filed with the clerk of the court in which the action is brought and by sending copies of the process and complaint, by registered mail, or by certified mail, to the Attorney General of the United States at Washington, District of Columbia. In such actions the United States may appear and answer, plead or demur within sixty days after such service or such further time as the court may allow.

FORM 22. ATTORNEY FOR DEFENDANT IN ARMED SERVICES

STATE OF NORTH CAROLINA

COUNTY OF ______________________

File # ___________________________

In the General Court of Justice

____________________ Court Division

____

Plaintiff

vs.

MOTION FOR APPOINTMENT

OF ATTORNEY

____

Defendant(s)

Now comes _______________________________, attorney for the plaintiff in the above-entitled action, and makes known to the court that __________________________, defendant in the action, is [may be] a member of the armed services and has been duly served with summons.

Wherefore, in accordance with the Soldiers' and Sailors' Civil Relief Act, 50 U.S.C. App. § 520, motion is hereby made to the court to appoint ___________________________ attorney for the defendant to represent him or her in this action.

This _________ day of __________________________, ______.

____

Attorney for the Plaintiff

____

Address

____

Telephone

Because some federal statutes subordinate liens held by federal agencies [including tax liens, Int. Rev. Code of 1986, § 6323 (b)(6), and Small Business Administration liens, 15 U.S.C. § 646] to local property tax liens, the redemption provisions of 28 U.S.C. § 2410(c) may become relevant:

> Where a sale of real estate is made to satisfy a lien prior to that of the United States, the United States shall have one year from the date of sale within which to redeem, except that with respect to a lien arising under the internal revenue laws the period shall be 120 days or the period allowable for redemption under state law, whichever is longer, and in any case in which, under the provisions of section 505 of the Housing Act of 1950, as amended (12 U.S.C. 1701k), and subsection (d) of section 1820 of title 38 of the United States Code, the right to redeem does not arise, there shall be no right of redemption.

FORM 23. APPOINTMENT OF ATTORNEY

STATE OF NORTH CAROLINA

COUNTY OF _______________________

File # _________________________________

In the General Court of Justice

_____________________ Court Division

____

Plaintiff

vs.

ORDER APPOINTING ATTORNEY

____

Defendant(s)

It appearing from motion of _____________________, attorney for the plaintiff in the above-entitled action, that _____________________, defendant, may be a member of the armed services, and that _____________________, who is found by the court to be an attorney licensed to practice before the courts of this state, has come into court and signified his or her willingness to accept appointment as attorney for the defendant;

It is therefore ordered that _____________________be appointed attorney for _____________________, defendant in this action.

This __________ day of _____________________, ______.

____

_____________________ of the

_____________________ Court

Appointment accepted.

____

Attorney

____

Address

____

Telephone

____

Date

ANSWER OF THE TAXING UNIT MADE DEFENDANT

Under the provisions of G.S. 105-374(c), "all other taxing units having tax liens" against the real property to be foreclosed must be made parties defendant in the action. Form 24 is a guide in preparing a defendant taxing unit's answer.

G.S. 105-374(h) has this to say about the answer:

> The liens of any taxing unit made a party defendant in any foreclosure action shall be alleged in an answer filed by the taxing unit, and the tax collector of each such answering unit shall, prior to judgment ordering sale, file a certificate of subsequent taxes similar to that filed by the tax collector of the plaintiff unit, and the taxes of each answering unit shall be of equal dignity with the taxes of the plaintiff unit. Any answering unit may, in case of payment of the plaintiff unit's taxes, continue the foreclosure action until all taxes due to it have been paid, and it shall not be necessary for any answering unit to file a separate foreclosure action or to proceed under G.S. 105-375 with respect to any such taxes.

Ordinarily, a defendant taxing unit would be justified in admitting the allegations of the complaint and joining in the prayer for relief, except that it should ask that its tax lien be adjudged to be on a parity with that of the plaintiff unit's. In answering the paragraph of the complaint that refers to it (Paragraph 3), the defendant taxing unit should set up its claim for taxes in the same way the plaintiff unit did in the complaint. It should further insert an allegation concerning subsequent taxes as a basis for later presentation of the certificate of taxes due.

If a taxing unit made defendant in a foreclosure action fails to file an answer and certificate of subsequent taxes, the third paragraph of G.S. 105-374(h) becomes pertinent:

> If a taxing unit properly served as a party defendant in a foreclosure action fails to answer and file the certificate provided for in the preceding paragraph, all of its taxes shall be barred by the judgment of sale except to the extent that the purchase price at the foreclosure sale (after payment of costs and of the liens of all taxing units whose liens are properly alleged by complaint or answer and certificates) may be sufficient to pay such taxes. However, if a defendant taxing unit is plaintiff in another foreclosure action pending against the same property, or if it has begun a proceeding under § 105-375, its answer may allege that fact in lieu of alleging its liens, and the court, in its discretion, may order consolidation of such actions or such other disposition thereof (and such disposition of the costs therein) as it may deem

FORM 24. ANSWER OF THE TAXING UNIT MADE DEFENDANT

STATE OF NORTH CAROLINA

COUNTY OF _______________________

File # _________________________

In the General Court of Justice

_____________________ Court Division

____

Plaintiff

vs.

ANSWER

____

Defendant(s)

The defendant, ____________________________, answering the complaint of the plaintiff, says:

1.   That the allegations contained in paragraphs 1, 2, 3, 4, 5, 6, and 7 of the complaint are not denied, except that this defendant says that, under the provisions of Section 105-356(a)(2) of the General Statutes, its lien for taxes due it on the property described in the complaint is on a parity with and of equal dignity with that of the plaintiff.

2.   Further answering the allegations in paragraph 3 of the complaint, this defendant says that it is a body politic and a duly organized and existing political subdivision of the State of North Carolina; that it lawfully assessed and levied taxes on the property described in the complaint in the years and for the amounts set out below, which taxes so levied and assessed, with penalties, interest, and costs allowed by law, are now due the defendant, _______________________________, and are on a parity with and of equal dignity with the lien of the plaintiff, and are superior to all other assessments, charges, rights, liens, and claims of any kind in and to the property described in the complaint, no part of the taxes having been paid:

Year	Principal amount of taxes, plus penalties and interest
_______	$______________
_______	$______________
Total due	$______________

That taxes for subsequent years may accrue or come due upon the property before the termination of this action; that such subsequently accruing taxes also constitute a lien upon the property; that this defendant will present to the court the certificate of the tax collector for [insert name of defendant taxing unit] with respect to such taxes at the time judgment is prayed herein and will ask that such subsequent taxes be included in the judgment.

Wherefore, this defendant asks that it be adjudged that the defendant have a lien for the

Form continues on next page. →

FORM 24. ANSWER OF THE TAXING UNIT MADE DEFENDANT (CONTINUED)

Wherefore, this defendant asks that it be adjudged that the defendant have a lien for the amount of taxes set forth herein, together with penalties, interest, and costs allowed by law, and that the lien be on a parity with and equal to the lien of the plaintiff and superior to all other claims and liens; that the taxes be paid from the proceeds of sale of the property; and that this defendant have such other and further relief as may be just and equitable.

____
Attorney for the Defendant

____
Address

____
Telephone

STATE OF NORTH CAROLINA
COUNTY OF _______________________

_______________________________, being sworn, says that he is the tax collector for the defendant taxing unit in the above-entitled action; that he has read the foregoing answer and knows the contents thereof; and that the same is true of his own knowledge, except as to matters therein stated to be alleged on information and belief, and as to those matters he believes them to be true.

____
Tax Collector

Sworn to and subscribed before me, this _________ day of _________________, _________.

____
(Signature of officer authorized
to administer oaths)

advisable. Any such order may be made by the clerk of the superior court subject to appeal in the same manner as appeals are taken from other orders of the clerk.

Thus a defendant taxing unit that fails to answer will risk receiving only the surplus, without the equality in the proceeds it would have had if it had answered properly.

If the taxing unit made a party defendant has already instituted a mortgage type of foreclosure action against the property under G.S. 105-374, G.S. 105-374(h) authorizes the court to order consolidation or other disposition of the action. Apparently, nothing is to be gained from maintaining two separate actions, and additional, unnecessary expenses are incurred. The attorney for the defendant taxing unit should inform the court of the previously commenced foreclosure action and move for consolidation of the suits under authority of G.S. 105-374(h).

When the defendant taxing unit has previously commenced an *in rem* foreclosure action under G.S. 105-375, a different situation is presented. The theories underlying the two types of actions are quite different, and certain requirements in the G.S. 105-374 procedures are not involved in the *in rem* procedure. Therefore, a unit that had commenced an action under G.S. 105-375 by docketing its lien certificate as a judgment would probably resist having its action consolidated with that of another taxing unit under G.S. 105-374. The defendant unit's attorney should move that its separate action be allowed to continue, and the court should so order. The actions could be consolidated for purposes of sale, however, as long as the order of sale makes clear that two separate judgments are being satisfied.

JUDGMENT ON TRIAL OF THE ISSUES
Under G.S. 105-374(k), the judgment in a foreclosure action should

> order the sale of the real property, or so much thereof as may be necessary for the satisfaction of: (1) taxes adjudged to be liens in favor of the plaintiff (other than taxes the amount of which has not been definitely determined) together with penalties, interest, and costs thereon; and (2) taxes adjudged to be liens in favor of other taxing units (other than taxes the amount of which has not yet been definitely determined) if those taxes have been alleged in answers filed by the other taxing units, together with penalties, interest, and costs thereon.

The same statute provides that the judgment "shall appoint a commissioner to conduct the sale and shall order that the property be sold in fee simple, free and clear of all interests, rights, claims and liens whatever. . . ."

The judgment should cover the costs of the action as well as the taxes, penalties, and interest. G.S. 105-374(i) states that the word "costs" shall include:

1. one reasonable attorney's fee for the plaintiff in such amount as the court shall, in its discretion, determine;[16]
2. an attorney's fee for any taxing unit joined as defendant "in such amount as the court shall, in its discretion, determine and allow"; and
3. a commissioner's fee to be fixed by the court, not exceeding 5 percent of the purchase price paid at the commissioner's sale.[17]

Under the terms of G.S. 105-374(i), the "governing body of any plaintiff unit may request the court to appoint as commissioner a salaried official, attorney, or employee of the unit and, when the requested appointment is made, may require that such commissioner's fees, when collected, be paid to plaintiff unit for its use."

Contests in tax foreclosure actions are rare, but this form is included for completeness. Any anticipation of defenses and issues that might arise in contested actions is beyond the scope of this book.

Note that Form 25 (as well as Forms 27 and 33) is drawn to declare a lien against the property rather than to render a money judgment against the defendants. This is in accordance with the theory of a tax foreclosure action as an action *quasi in rem* (see G.S. 1-75.8). Furthermore, as a matter of practice the property is usually sold for at least the amount of the judgment. Thus, tax foreclosure judgments

---

16. N.C. Gen. Stat. § 105-374(i) further provides: "The governing body of any taxing unit may, in its discretion, pay a smaller or greater sum than that allowed as costs to its attorney as a suit fee, and the governing body may allow a reasonable commission to its attorney on taxes collected by him after they have been placed in his hands; or the governing body may arrange with its attorney for the handling of tax foreclosure suits on a salary basis or may make any other reasonable agreement with its attorney or attorneys. Any arrangement made between a taxing unit and its attorney may provide that attorneys' fees collected as costs in foreclosure actions be collected for the use of the taxing unit."

17. "In case more than one sale is made of the same property in any action, the commissioner's fee may be based on the highest amount bid, but said commissioner shall not be allowed a separate fee for each such sale." N.C. Gen. Stat. § 105-374(i).

FORM 25. JUDGMENT ON TRIAL OF THE ISSUES

STATE OF NORTH CAROLINA

COUNTY OF _____________________

File # ________________________________

In the General Court of Justice

___________________________ Court Division

____

Plaintiff

vs.   JUDGMENT

____

Defendant(s)

This cause was heard before the undersigned judge of the court [and a jury], and it appearing to the court that this is an action to foreclose a lien for taxes due plaintiff upon the real property described in the complaint, and issues having been submitted to the jury and answered as follows:

[set out issues and answers];

It is therefore ordered and adjudged that the plaintiff has a first and prior lien upon the parcel or tract of real property described below for taxes for the following years and in the following amounts, together with the costs of this action:

Year   Amount (including interest)

_______ $______________

_______ $______________

_______ $______________

Total taxes and interest due $______________

That the real property upon which this judgment is a lien is located in _____________________________ Township, _____________________________ County, North Carolina, and is more particularly described as follows:

[copy full legal description from complaint].

And all of the right, title, and interest of the defendant in and to the real property is hereby barred and forever foreclosed, except as to his or her rights to redeem before confirmation of the sale and to participate in the distribution of any surplus resulting from the sale herein authorized in accordance with his or her relative claims thereto.

Form continues on next page. →

FORM 25. JUDGMENT ON TRIAL OF THE ISSUES (CONTINUED)

It is further ordered and adjudged that ___________________________ be appointed commissioner to sell the real property at public auction for cash to the highest bidder, at the courthouse door in ___________________________ County, after first posting notice of the sale at the courthouse in ___________________________ County for thirty days preceding the sale, and also advertising once a week for four successive weeks in some newspaper published in ___________________________ County [or, if no newspaper is published in the county, by advertising once a week for four successive weeks in some newspaper having a general circulation in the county]; and the commissioner shall sell the real property free and clear of all interests, rights, claims, and liens whatever except ad valorem taxes the amount of which cannot be determined and the taxes and assessments of taxing units that are not parties to this action; and the commissioner shall, within three days after the sale, make a report thereof to this court. A cash deposit of 5 percent of the highest bid shall be required on the sale at public auction, unless the highest bid is by a taxing unit; then a deposit shall not be required.

It is further ordered and adjudged that after delivery of the deed and collection of the purchase price, the commissioner shall apply the proceeds as provided by law.

The court further orders that a reasonable commissioner's fee not to exceed 5 percent of the purchase price and a reasonable attorney's fee for the plaintiff are to be determined at a later date, and that the costs of this action be recovered by the plaintiff.

And this cause is remanded to the clerk of this court for further proceedings in accordance with this judgment and the law provided in such cases.

This ___________ day of _______________________________, _______.

____
Judge Presiding

should declare a lien on the property and not impose a personal liability on the defendants.[18]

JUDGMENT ON THE PLEADINGS

In many (perhaps most) tax foreclosure actions under G.S. 105-374, the judgment obtained will be neither on trial of the issues nor by default but will instead be a judgment on the pleadings. Under Rule 12(c) of the Rules of Civil Procedure, a motion for a judgment on the pleadings would appear to be proper when the defendant has filed an answer but has not contested the action or attempted to deny any of the complaint's

18. Apex v. Templeton, 223 N.C. 645, 27 S.E.2d 617 (1943). *See also* City of Charlotte v. Little-McMahan Properties, Inc., 52 N.C. App. 464, 279 S.E.2d 104 (1981).

FORM 26. MOTION FOR JUDGMENT ON THE PLEADINGS

STATE OF NORTH CAROLINA

COUNTY OF _________________________

File # _________________________

In the General Court of Justice

__________________ Court Division

____

Plaintiff

vs.   MOTION

____

Defendant(s)

Now comes __________________________, attorney for the plaintiff, and moves the court pursuant to Rule 12(c) of the Rules of Civil Procedure that judgment be entered for plaintiff on the pleadings as to the defendant _________________________, as it appears from the answer that no material issue of fact exists, and plaintiff is entitled to such judgment as a matter of law.

This _________ day of __________________________, ______.

____

Attorney for the Plaintiff

____

Address

____

Telephone

To: _____________________________, Defendant(s)

Attorney for _________________________

Please take notice that the undersigned will bring the above motion on for hearing before this court on the _________ day of ________________________, ______, at _____ ___.M., or as soon thereafter as the matter may be heard.

____

Attorney for the Plaintiff

____

Address

____

Telephone

FORM 27. JUDGMENT ON THE PLEADINGS

STATE OF NORTH CAROLINA   File # _________________________

COUNTY OF _________________________ In the General Court of Justice

               _________________________ Court Division

____

Plaintiff

vs.   JUDGMENT

____

Defendant(s)

   This matter was heard before the undersigned _________________________ of the _________________________ Court, upon motion of plaintiff for judgment on the pleadings and it appearing to the court that this is an action for the foreclosure of the lien for taxes due the plaintiff upon real property described in the complaint and it further appearing to the court that plaintiff, at the time of the institution of this action, filed a complaint setting out the amount of its tax lien against the property, and now files a proper certificate showing the amount of taxes that have subsequently accrued against the property, as authorized by G.S. 105-374(c); and it further appearing that the defendant named in this action has been properly served with summons and _________________________, defendant, has duly filed an answer to the complaint that admits the allegations contained therein and does not contest the amount owed and sought to be recovered, or plaintiff's right to foreclose the liens on the property described therein, or in any other manner deny or contest the allegations contained therein:

   It is therefore ordered and adjudged upon motion of _________________________, attorney for the plaintiff, that the plaintiff has a first and prior lien upon the parcel or tract of real property described below for taxes for the following years and in the following amounts, together with the costs of this action:

Year	Amount (including interest)
_______	$_____________
_______	$_____________
Total taxes and interest due	$_____________

   That the real property upon which this judgment is a lien is located in _________________________ Township, _________________________ County, North Carolina, and is more particularly described as follows:

allegations. This would occur, for example, when a defendant taxing unit has filed an answer asserting its own liens or when a guardian *ad litem* has filed an answer admitting the allegations of the complaint. G.S. 105-374(k) expressly provides that when the answers filed do not seek to pre-

FORM 27. JUDGMENT ON THE PLEADINGS

[copy full legal description from complaint].

And all of the right, title, and interest of the defendant in and to the property are hereby barred and forever foreclosed, except as to his or her rights to redeem before confirmation of the sale and to participate in the distribution of any surplus resulting from the sale herein authorized in accordance with his or her relative claims thereto.

It is further ordered and adjudged that _______________________________ be appointed commissioner to sell the real property at public auction for cash to the highest bidder, at the courthouse door in _______________________________ County, after first posting notice of said sale at the courthouse in _______________________________ County for thirty days preceding the sale, and also advertising once a week for four successive weeks in some newspaper published in _______________________________ County [or, if no newspaper is published in the county, by advertising once a week for four successive weeks in a newspaper having a general circulation in the county]; and the commissioner shall sell the real property free and clear of all interests, rights, claims, and liens whatever except ad valorem taxes the amount of which cannot be determined and the taxes and assessments of taxing units that are not parties to this action; and the commissioner shall, within three days after the sale, make a report thereof to this Court. A cash deposit of 5 percent of the highest bid shall be required on the sale at public auction, unless the highest bid is by a taxing unit; then a deposit shall not be required.

It is further ordered and adjudged that after delivery of the deed and collection of the purchase price, the commissioner shall apply the proceeds as provided by law.

The court further orders that a reasonable commissioner's fee not to exceed 5 percent of the purchase price and a reasonable attorney's fee for the plaintiff are to be determined at a later date, and that the costs of this action be recovered by the plaintiff.

And this cause is retained for further orders.

This _____________ day of _______________________________, _______.

____
Clerk of Superior Court

vent the sale of the property, the clerk of superior court may render the judgment. Form 26 is for the motion for judgment on the pleadings, and Form 27 is for the judgment itself.

JUDGMENT BY DEFAULT

G.S. 1A-1, Rule 55(b)(1), provides that the clerk of court may enter judgment by default when the defendant "has been defaulted for failure to appear and if he is not an infant or incompetent person"; in all other cases application must be made to the judge for judgment by default. G.S. 105-374(k), however, provides that "[i]n all cases in which no answer is filed within the time allowed by law, and in cases in which answers filed do not seek to prevent sale of said property, the clerk of the superior court may render the judgment, subject to appeal in the same manner as appeals are taken from other judgments of the clerk." Thus, G.S. 105-374(k) appears to create an exception to the general rule of G.S. 1A-1, Rule 55(b)(1), for tax lien foreclosure cases to authorize the clerk to enter a default judgment in cases where the defendants may be infants or incompetents. The following forms are written for entry of judgment by the clerk, but in counties in which the clerk insists on a strict application of G.S. 1A-1, Rule 55(b)(1), the judge will have to enter the judgment. If the defendant against whom the default judgment is sought has made an appearance in the action, either personally or by representative, the defendant or his or her representative must be served with notice of the application for judgment by default at least three days before the hearing on the application takes place.

Under G.S. 1A-1, Rule 55, a two-stage process is required for entering a default judgment: first, the clerk must make an entry of default, and second, either the clerk or judge must render the judgment by default. Form 28 is for the motion to the clerk to make the entry of default. Form 29 is for the affidavit that must be presented to the clerk, including both the statement of jurisdiction required by G.S. 1-75.11(2) and the assertion of default. Form 30 is for the entry of default by the clerk. See also Forms 9, 12, and 14 for proof-of-service affidavits that must be filed before judgment by default may be obtained.

G.S. 1A-1, Rule 55(b)(1), provides that the amount due may be presented to the court either by affidavit or by verified complaint. If the foreclosure complaint is verified, as recommended in Form 7, it will serve this purpose.

Form 31 is for the affidavit and motion for default judgment by the clerk. Form 32 is for the default judgment. G.S. 1A-1, Rule 54(c), provides that a default judgment "shall not be different in kind from or exceed in amount that prayed for in the demand for judgment."

If any of the defendants against whom the default judgment is sought are in military service, or if the plaintiff's attorney is unable to determine whether any of them are in military service, Forms 21, 22, and 23 should be used to appoint an attorney for these defendants.

FORM **28.** MOTION FOR ENTRY OF DEFAULT

STATE OF NORTH CAROLINA

COUNTY OF _______________________

File # _______________________________

In the General Court of Justice

_______________________ Court Division

____

Plaintiff

vs.

MOTION FOR ENTRY

OF DEFAULT

____

Defendant(s)

    Now comes _______________________________, attorney for the plaintiff in the above-entitled action, and moves the court pursuant to Rule 55(a) of the Rules of Civil Procedure to enter the default of defendant _______________________________, and plaintiff respectfully shows the court that the defendant has failed to plead or is otherwise subject to default judgment as provided by the Rules of Civil Procedure or by statute as shown by the affidavit attached hereto.

    This __________ day of _______________________, ______.

____

Attorney for the Plaintiff

____

Address

____

Telephone

FORM 29. AFFIDAVIT OF JURISDICTION AND FAILURE TO PLEAD

STATE OF NORTH CAROLINA

COUNTY OF _______________________

File # _______________________

In the General Court of Justice

_______________________ Court Division

Plaintiff

vs.

Defendant(s)

AFFIDAVIT OF JURISDICTION
AND FAILURE TO PLEAD

_______________________, being sworn, says:

1.   That in the above-entitled action now pending in the Court of _______________ County, he or she is attorney for the plaintiff;

2.   That the above-entitled action to foreclose the liens for taxes owed the [City] [County] of _______________________________ was commenced on the _______ day of _______________, _______, against real property located in _______________ County, _______________ Township, and more particularly described in the complaint filed in the action;

3.   That the defendant, whose last known address is _______________, has an interest in the real property that is the subject of this foreclosure action and was served with process according to G.S. 1A-1, Rule 4 by [personal service] [registered or certified mail] [publication], as shown by the attached proof of service affidavits;

4.   That jurisdiction *quasi in rem* within the terms of G.S. 1-75.8 was acquired over the defendant by service of process in the manner described above;

5.   That the time for filing answer or other pleading by defendant has expired and no answer or other pleading has been filed by defendant, and defendant has not otherwise appeared to defend the action.

6.   This affidavit is made pursuant to the requirements of G.S. 1-75.11(2) and G.S. 1A-1, Rule 55(a), for the purpose of obtaining an entry of default against the defendant named.

____
Attorney for the Plaintiff

____
Address

____
Telephone

Sworn to and subscribed before me, this _______________ day of _______________ _______________, _______.

____
(Signature of officer authorized to administer oaths)

FORM 30. ENTRY OF DEFAULT

STATE OF NORTH CAROLINA

COUNTY OF ________________________

File # ________________________________

In the General Court of Justice

______________________ Court Division

____

Plaintiff

vs.

ENTRY OF DEFAULT

____

Defendant(s)

That whereas it has been made to appear to the undersigned Clerk of the Superior Court of ________________________________ County, upon Affidavit, that the defendant [has failed to plead—or other basis for default];

And that the defendant is otherwise subject to default judgment as provided by the Rules of Civil Procedure;

Now, therefore, default is hereby entered against the defendant in this action as provided by Rule 55(a) of the Rules of Civil Procedure.

This __________ day of ________________________________, ________ at ____ ___.M.

____

Clerk of the Superior Court

FORM 31. MOTION FOR DEFAULT JUDGMENT

STATE OF NORTH CAROLINA

COUNTY OF _______________________

File # _________________________________

In the General Court of Justice

_______________________ Court Division

____

Plaintiff

vs.

____

Defendant(s)

MOTION FOR

DEFAULT JUDGMENT

Now comes________________________________, attorney for the plaintiff in the above-entitled action, and states:

That the complaint in the above cause was filed in this court on the ___________ day of _______________________________, _______;

That default was entered in the civil docket in the office of the clerk of superior court on the ___________ day of _________________________________, _______, and that no proceedings have been taken by the defendant since default was entered;

That the amount of taxes plus penalties and interest upon the real property described in the complaint of the above-entitled action is $___________, as shown by the verified complaint;

That _________________________________, defendant, has failed to appear, either personally or by representative;

That as will appear from the affidavit attached hereto as Appendix 1, defendant ___________ _______________________ is not a member of the armed forces;[19]

Wherefore, plaintiff moves that pursuant to Rule 55(b)(1) of the Rules of Civil Procedure, judgment by default be entered against _________________________________, defendant, for the foreclosure of its tax liens, as prayed in the complaint.

This ___________ day of _________________________________, _______.

____

Attorney for the Plaintiff

____

Address

____

Telephone

FORM 32. JUDGMENT BY DEFAULT

STATE OF NORTH CAROLINA

COUNTY OF _________________________

File # _________________________________

In the General Court of Justice

_____________________________ Court Division

____

Plaintiff

vs.

JUDGMENT

____

Defendant(s)

This matter was heard before the undersigned _______________________ of the _______________________________ Court, and it appearing to the court that this is an action for the foreclosure of the lien for taxes due the plaintiff upon real property described in the complaint, and it further appearing to the court that plaintiff, at the time of the institution of this action, filed a complaint setting out the amount of its tax lien against the real property, and now files a proper certificate showing the amount of taxes that have subsequently accrued against the real property, as authorized by Section 105- 374(e) of the General Statutes; and it further appearing that the defendant named in this action has been properly served with summons and that the time for answering the complaint of the plaintiff has expired as to the defendant, and that the defendant has not filed any answer or other pleading to this action;

It is therefore ordered and adjudged upon motion of ________________, attorney for the plaintiff, that the plaintiff has a first and prior lien upon the parcel or tract of real property described below for taxes for the following years and in the following amounts, together with costs of this action:

Year	Amount (including interest)
_______	$________________
_______	$________________
Total taxes and interest due	$________________

That the real property upon which this judgment is a lien is located in _______________________ Township, _________________________________ County, North Carolina, and is more particularly described as follows:

Form continues on next page. →

19. See Form 21.

FORM 32. JUDGMENT BY DEFAULT (CONTINUED)

[copy full legal description from complaint].

And all of the right, title, and interest of the defendant in and to the real property are hereby barred and forever foreclosed, except as to his or her rights to redeem before confirmation of the sale and to participate in the distribution of any surplus resulting from the sale herein authorized in accordance with his or her relative claims thereto.

It is further ordered and adjudged that ____________________ is appointed commissioner to sell the real property at public auction for cash to the highest bidder, at the courthouse door in __________________ County, after first posting notice of the sale at the courthouse in __________________ County for thirty days preceding the sale, and also advertising once a week for four successive weeks in some newspaper published in ____________________ County [or, if no newspaper is published in the county, by advertising for four successive weeks in a newspaper having a general circulation in the county]; and the commissioner shall sell the real property free and clear of all interests, rights, claims, and liens whatever except ad valorem taxes the amount of which cannot be determined and the taxes and assessments of taxing units not parties to this action; and the commissioner shall, within three days after the sale, make a report thereof to this court. A cash deposit of 5 percent of the highest bid shall be required on the sale at public auction unless the highest bid is by a taxing unit; then a deposit shall not be required.

It is further ordered and adjudged that after delivery of the deed and collection of the purchase price, the commissioner shall apply the proceeds as provided by law.

The court further orders that a reasonable commissioner's fee not to exceed 5 percent of the purchase price and a reasonable attorney's fee for the plaintiff are to be determined at a later date, and that the costs of this action are to be recovered by the plaintiff.

And this cause is retained for further orders.

This __________ day of ___________________________, ______.

____

___________________________ of the

___________________________ Court

DISMISSAL OF THE FORECLOSURE ACTION

If the defendant pays all taxes, interest, and costs (including the costs of the foreclosure action) before the conclusion of the suit, the plaintiff should have the action dismissed. The action can be dismissed at any time before the plaintiff has rested its case by filing a notice of dismissal with the court, as follows in Form 33. Among the costs that must be paid before an action is dismissed are attorney's fees. G.S. 105-374(i) provides that one attorney's fee shall be included as costs as the court shall "determine and allow." In most cases in which an action is dismissed, the taxpayer, or someone on behalf of the taxpayer, will pay the attorney's fee along with the costs and other taxes. In situations in which the taxpayer balks at paying the fee, however, the fee must be allowed by the court. Form 34 is for the motion for allowance of the fee, and Form 35 is for the order allowing the fee.

After the plaintiff has rested its case, the action can be dismissed only by the filing of a stipulation of dismissal signed by all of the parties that have appeared in the action or by order of the judge on motion by the plaintiff. Form 36 is for the motion to dismiss, and Form 37 is for the order of dismissal.

As indicated in these last two forms, a dismissal should not be taken unless the defendant pays all of the taxes shown in the complaint, together with the costs of the action. Since the costs are taxed against the plaintiff unit, the plaintiff's attorney should get a final statement of costs before accepting settlement and having the action dismissed. Ordinarily, once the suit is started the attorney should require payment of all delinquent taxes before obtaining dismissal; otherwise he or she may have to bring suit again. If the defendant wants to pay only a part of the amount due and promises to pay the balance later, the attorney can agree not to pray judgment if the balance is paid by a certain date. Or he may proceed to judgment on an understanding that the sale will not be made if the balance is paid by the date promised.

FORM 33. VOLUNTARY DISMISSAL OF ACTION

STATE OF NORTH CAROLINA   File # _______________________

COUNTY OF _____________________   In the General Court of Justice

_____________________ Court Division

____

Plaintiff

vs.   NOTICE OF DISMISSAL

____

Defendant(s)

Notice is hereby given that the plaintiff voluntarily dismisses this action pursuant to G.S. 1A-1, Rule 41(a)(1), without prejudice.

This __________ day of _______________________________, ________.

____

Attorney for the Plaintiff

____

Address

____

Telephone

FORM 34. MOTION FOR ALLOWANCE OF ATTORNEY'S FEE

STATE OF NORTH CAROLINA

COUNTY OF ___________________________

File # _________________________________

In the General Court of Justice

_______________________ Court Division

____

Plaintiff

vs.

MOTION FOR ALLOWANCE
OF ATTORNEY'S FEE

____

Defendant(s)

       Pursuant to North Carolina General Statutes, Section 105–374(i), the undersigned attorney for the plaintiff shows the court that he or she has performed the services in this action listed in Attachment 1 and prays that a fee of \$________________ be allowed as reasonable.

____

Attorney for the Plaintiff

____

Address

____

Telephone

FORM 35. ORDER ALLOWING ATTORNEY'S FEE

STATE OF NORTH CAROLINA

COUNTY OF _______________________

File # _______________________________

In the General Court of Justice

_______________________ Court Division

____

Plaintiff

vs.

ORDER ALLOWING
ATTORNEY'S FEE

____

Defendant(s)

On motion of the attorney for the plaintiff the court finds that the attorney has rendered services in this action and that a fee of $_________________ is reasonable compensation for those services and is allowed.

This __________ day of _______________________________, ______.

____

_______________________________ of the

_______________________________ Court

FORM **36.** MOTION TO DISMISS

STATE OF NORTH CAROLINA

COUNTY OF _______________________

File # _______________________

In the General Court of Justice

_______________________ Court Division

____

Plaintiff

vs.

MOTION TO DISMISS

____

Defendant(s)

Now comes _______________________, attorney for the plaintiff in the above-entitled action, and states:

That plaintiff's lien for taxes, as set forth in the complaint, and the costs of this action, as shown below, have been fully paid and satisfied:

Year	Amount (including interest)
______	$______
______	$______
______	$______
Subtotal	$______
Costs (including attorney's fee of $______)	$______
Total	$______

Wherefore plaintiff moves this court that plaintiff's action against defendant be dismissed pursuant to Rule 41(a)(2) of the Rules of Civil Procedure, without prejudice.

This __________ day of _______________________, ______.

____

Attorney for the Plaintiff

____

Address

____

Telephone

FORM 37. ORDER OF DISMISSAL

STATE OF NORTH CAROLINA

File # ____________________________

COUNTY OF ________________________

In the General Court of Justice

_________________________ Court Division

____

Plaintiff

vs.

ORDER OF DISMISSAL

____

Defendant(s)

This matter being heard before the undersigned ____________________ of the ____________________ Court, and it appearing to the court that plaintiff's lien for taxes as set out in the complaint and the costs of this action have been fully paid and satisfied;

It is, upon motion of __________________________, attorney for the plaintiff, ordered that plaintiff take nothing by this action and that this action be dismissed without prejudice.

It is further ordered that the costs of this action be taxed against the plaintiff.

This __________ day of __________________________, ______.

____

____________________________ of the

____________________________ Court

COMPROMISE

Although compromises of tax claims are rarely permissible, there may be situations in which the attorney desires to obtain a dismissal upon payment of less than the full amount of delinquent taxes. Before agreeing to a compromise, the attorney should obtain approval of the unit's governing board and have the authorization for the compromise entered in the board's official minutes.

In such a situation Form 38 should be substituted for Form 37.

FORM 38. COMPROMISE

<table>
<tr><td>

STATE OF NORTH CAROLINA

COUNTY OF _______________________

____

Plaintiff

vs.

____

Defendant(s)

</td><td>

File # ___________________________

In the General Court of Justice

______________________ Court Division

ORDER OF DISMISSAL

</td></tr>
</table>

This matter being heard before the undersigned __________________________ of the __________________________ Court, and it appearing to the court that plaintiff's lien for taxes as set out in the complaint and the costs of this action have been fully paid and satisfied;

It is, upon motion of __________________________, attorney for the plaintiff, ordered that this action be, and it is hereby, dismissed without prejudice, and plaintiff is taxed with the costs.

This _________ day of __________________________, ______.

____

Judge of the __________________________ Court

CERTIFICATE OF TAXES DUE
G.S. 105-374(e) provides:

The complaint in a tax foreclosure action brought under this section by a taxing unit shall, in addition to alleging the tax lien on which the action is based, include a general allegation of subsequent taxes which are or may become a lien on the same property in favor of the plaintiff unit .... In case of redemption before confirmation of the foreclosure sale, the person redeeming shall be required to pay, before the foreclosure action is discontinued, at least all taxes on the real property which have at the time of discontinuance become due to the plaintiff unit, plus penalties, interest and costs thereon. Immediately prior to judgment ordering sale in a foreclosure action (if there has been no redemption prior to that time), the tax collector or the attorney for the plaintiff unit shall file in the action a certificate (Form 39) setting forth all taxes which are a lien on the real property in favor of the plaintiff unit (other than taxes the amount of which has not been definitely determined).

FORM 39. CERTIFICATE OF TAXES DUE

STATE OF NORTH CAROLINA

COUNTY OF ________________________

File # ________________________________

In the General Court of Justice

________________________________ Court Division

____

Plaintiff

vs.

CERTIFICATE

____

Defendant(s)

To the Honorable ________________________________, Clerk of Superior Court of ________________________ County:

Now comes________________________________, tax collector for the plaintiff taxing unit in the above-entitled action, and certifies that the following taxes are liens in favor of the plaintiff on the property that is the subject of this action:

Year	Amount (including interest)
______	$______________
______	$______________
______	$______________
Total taxes and interest due	$______________

This certificate is filed pursuant to G.S. 105-374(e).

This __________ day of ________________________________, ______.

____

Tax Collector

This statute provides an easy way for the taxing unit to include in the final judgment taxes and interest that accrue between the action's start and the final judgment. Several months may have elapsed between the complaint's filing and the judgment. The taxing unit will want to include the interest for these months in the judgment, in addition to any subsequent taxes that may have accrued, and the procedure for doing so is the filing of a certificate of taxes due. A general allegation as to subsequent taxes may be included in the complaint, and the certificate, the form for which is set out here, must be filed just before judgment.

Under G.S. 105-374(h), a defendant taxing unit should follow the same procedure.

NOTICE OF SALE

G.S. 105-374(1) provides that the foreclosure sale must be advertised in the manner provided by Article 29A of Chapter 1 of the General Statutes. Several sections of Article 29A apply.

The time for beginning the required advertisement (Form 40) is set out in G.S. 1-339.16: "An order of sale may provide for the beginning of the advertisement of sale at any time after the order is issued. If the order does not specify such time, the advertisement may be begun at any time after the order is issued." To comply with G.S. 1-339.17(b)(2), the advertisement should be *last* published in a newspaper within ten days of the sale date.

G.S. 1-339.15 provides what must be included in the notice. The notice shall

1. refer to the order authorizing the sale;
2. designate the date, hour, and place of sale;
3. describe the real property to be sold, by reference or otherwise, sufficiently to identify it, and add such further description as will acquaint bidders with the nature and location of the property;

[4. deleted]

5. state the terms of the sale, specifying the amount of the cash deposit, if any, to be made by the highest bidder at the sale; and
6. include any other provisions required by the order of sale.

G.S. 1-339.17 prescribes the manner in which the advertising is to be conducted:

a. Subject to subsection (d) of this section, notice of public sale of real property shall:
    1. Be posted, in the area designated by the clerk of superior court for posting notices in the county in which the

FORM 40. GENERAL NOTICE OF TAX FORECLOSURE SALE

Under and by virtue of an order of the _________________________ Court of _________________ County, North Carolina, made and entered in the action entitled "_________________ vs. _________________," the undersigned commissioner will on the _________ day of _________________, _____, offer for sale and sell for cash, to the last and highest bidder at public auction, at the courthouse door in _________________ County, North Carolina, in _________________ at 12:00 noon the following described real property, lying and being in _________________ Township, State and County aforesaid, and more particularly described as follows:

[copy full legal description from the complaint or use a tax map or other brief description].

The sale will be made subject to all outstanding city and county taxes and all local improvement assessments against the above-described property not included in the judgment in the above-entitled cause. A deposit of 5 percent of the successful bid will be required.

This _________ day of _________________, _____.

____
Commissioner

---

property is situated, for at least 20 days immediately preceding the sale; and

  2. Be published once a week for at least two successive weeks:

    a. In a newspaper qualified for legal advertising published in the county; or

    b. if no newspaper qualified for legal advertising is published in the county, in a newspaper having general circulation in the county.

 b. When the notice of public sale is published in a newspaper,

    1. The period from the date of the first publication to the date of the last publication, both dates inclusive, shall not be less than seven days, including Sundays, and

    2. The date of the last publication shall not be more than 10 days preceding the date of sale in a sale by auction or the date on which sealed bids are opened in a sale by sealed bids.

This statute also provides that if the real property to be sold is in more than one county, the provisions of subsections (a) and (b) above must be complied with in each county in which any part of the property is situated. Finally, it provides that in addition to the requirements listed above, the notice of the sale must be otherwise posted or the sale must be otherwise advertised as the judge or clerk may require.

If a deposit is to be required from the bidder, authority for the requirement should be inserted in the judgment and also shown on the notice of sale. A requirement of a deposit of 5 percent of the bid has been included in the judgments in this book. Attorneys bringing foreclosure actions may wish to increase this amount or eliminate the deposit requirement altogether.

A copy of the newspaper advertisement attached to the publisher's affidavit of publication (and of any advertisements of resales) should be filed with the papers in the case.

Some attorneys have found it useful to mail copies of the notice of sale to real estate agents and other persons who have expressed an interest in bidding on property at foreclosure sales.

PLACING A SIGN ON THE PROPERTY

In addition to the legally required advertising and the mailing of letters or notices to the owners and other defendants, attorneys for a number of taxing units have found it helpful to place a large sign on the property to be sold. The sign serves several purposes. It alerts adjacent property owners and other landowners in the neighborhood of the sale, and they are often good prospective bidders. It also, on occasion, turns up an heir or other person with a legal interest in the property, hitherto not found, who will pay the taxes before the property is sold.

A typical sign is:

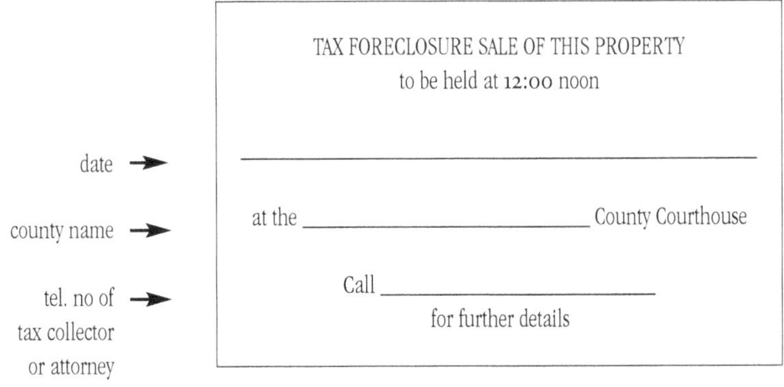

FORM **41.** NOTICE OF SALE TO OWNER

Dear Sir or Madam:

This is to notify you that the real estate listed for taxes in the name of
________________________________ and described as

[insert a description sufficient to identify the property]

is to be sold for delinquent taxes at the courthouse door in ________________________________
County, at 12:00 noon on the __________ day of ____,
__________, under order ________ of the ______________________________________ Court of
____ County, North Carolina, made and entered in the action
entitled "______________________________ vs. ________________________________."
If you wish to protect your interest in the above-described property, you should get in touch
with this office before the sale or else attend the sale itself.

Very truly yours,

____

Attorney for [City]

[County] of ________________________________

NOTICE OF SALE TO OWNER

The letter set out in Form 41 is not required, but sending it is in keeping
with a policy both of doing everything possible to collect the taxes rather
than sell the property and advising interested parties on the status of the
foreclosure proceeding. If used, the letter should be sent to record owners
and also to lienholders likely to protect their interests. In lieu of this letter,
some attorneys may wish to send copies of the notice of sale.

REPORT OF SALE

G.S. 105-374(n) requires the commissioner holding the sale to report it
to the court within three days following the sale, and Form 42 serves this
purpose.

FORM 42. REPORT OF SALE

STATE OF NORTH CAROLINA

COUNTY OF _______________________

File #

In the General Court of Justice

_________________________Court Division

Before the Clerk

____

Plaintiff

vs.

REPORT OF SALE

____

Defendant(s)

To the Honorable _______________________________, the Clerk of the Superior Court.

The undersigned, _______________________________, respectfully reports to the court:

That pursuant to the power and authority vested in me as commissioner under a judgment entered in this action by the Honorable _________________, of the _________________ Court of _______________________________ County, I offered for sale at public auction for cash to the last and highest bidder, on the ______ day of _____________________, ______, at 12:00 noon at the courthouse door in _______________________ County, the real property described in the judgment in this action after due advertisement of the sale in the manner prescribed by law, at which time and place _______________________________ became the last and highest bidder for the property for the amount of $_________________.

This ___________ day of _____________________________, ________.

____

Commissioner

UPSET BIDS

G.S. 105-374(o) provides that at any time within ten days after the commissioner's report of the original sale is filed, any person who has an interest in the property may file exceptions to the report, and that at any time within this ten-day period an increased or upset bid may be filed as provided by Article 29A of Chapter 1 of the General Statutes.

An upset bid is defined in G.S. 1-339.25(a) as

an advanced, increased or raised bid in a public sale by auction whereby a person offers to purchase real property theretofore sold for an amount exceeding the reported sale price or the last upset bid by a minimum of five percent (5%) thereof, but in any event with a minimum increase of seven hundred fifty dollars ($750.00). Subject to the provisions of subsection (A) of this section, an upset bid shall be made by delivering to the clerk of superior court with whom the report of the sale or the last notice of upset bid was filed, a deposit in cash or by certified check or cashier's check satisfactory to the clerk in an amount greater than or equal to five percent (5%) of the amount of the upset bid but in no event less than seven hundred fifty dollars ($750.00). The deposit required by this section shall be filed with the clerk of the superior court with whom the report of sale or the last notice of upset bid was filed, by the close of normal business hours on the tenth day after the filing of the report of sale or the last notice of upset bid, and if the tenth day shall fall upon a Sunday or legal holiday or upon a day in which the office of the clerk is not open for the regular dispatch of its business, the deposit may be made and the notice of upset bid may be filed on the day following when said office is open for the regular dispatch of its business. Except as provided in G.S. 1-339.27A and G.S. 1-339.30, there shall be no resales; however, there may be successive upset bids, each of which shall be followed by a period of 10 days for a further upset bid. If a timely motion for resale is filed under G.S. 1-339.27A, no upset bids may be filed while the motion is pending. If an upset bid or a motion for resale under G.S. 1-339.27A is not filed within 10 days following a sale, resale, or prior upset bid, the rights of the parties to the sale or resale become fixed.

G.S. 1-339.25(d1) requires a person making an upset bid to file a notice of upset bid with the clerk of superior court. The notice must:

1. State the name, address, and telephone number of the upset bidder;
2. Specify the amount of the upset bid;
3. Provide that the sale shall remain open for a period of 10 days after the bid on which the notice of upset bid is filed for the filing of additional upset bids as permitted by law; and
4. Be signed by the upset bidder or the attorney or the agent of the upset bidder.

When a proper upset has been made, G.S. 1-339.25(d2) requires the clerk of superior court to notify the commissioner, and the commissioner is then required to mail a written notice of the upset bid by first-class mail to the last known addresses of the last prior bidder and the current record owners of the property.

G.S. 1-339.25, as amended in 2001 and effective January 1, 2002, provides for successive upset bids and a resale only in the event that a motion for resale is made pursuant to G.S. 1-339.27A. The former practice of a motion for and order of resale after each upset bid has been eliminated. After ten days have expired following a sale, resale, or upset bid without another upset bid or motion for resale, the rights of the parties become fixed, and the the commissioner's next step is to move for confirmation of the sale. If one or more upset bids has been made, then the sale being confirmed is the sale based on the last upset bid. Form 44 is for the motion for confirmation, and Form 45 is for the judgment of confirmation.

ASSIGNMENT OF BID

G.S. 105-376(a) provides that a taxing unit that has bid on the property at the foreclosure sale "may assign its bid at any time, by private sale, for not less than the amount of the bid." An assignment (Form 43) made by the taxing unit should be signed in the unit's name by the chief executive officer—mayor or chair of the board of commissioners—and attested by the clerk to the board, with the seal affixed. Authority for making the assignment should appear in the board's minutes. Occasionally an attorney will question a title because an assignment of the bid does not appear in the foreclosure file.

FORM 43. ASSIGNMENT OF BID

STATE OF NORTH CAROLINA   File # _______________________

COUNTY OF _______________________   In the General Court of Justice

         _______________________ Court Division

_______________________________   Before the Clerk

Plaintiff

vs.   ASSIGNMENT

____

Defendant(s)

The [County] [City] of _______________________ was the last and highest bidder for that certain tract or parcel of real estate described in the judgment in the above-entitled cause at a sale held on the __________ day of _______________________, _______, and I, _______________________, as [Mayor of the city] [Chair of the Board of Commissioners of the county], pursuant to authority vested in me by resolution of the [City Council] [Board of County Commissioners] dated _______________________, _______, do hereby, in consideration of _______________________'s promise to pay the sum of $______________, the amount of the bid, to the commissioner upon confirmation of the sale, sell, set over, transfer and assign the [county's] [city's] bid made at the sale unto _______________________, his or her heirs and assigns; and _______________________, commissioner in the sale, is hereby instructed to execute and deliver a deed conveying the real property to _______________________, his or her heirs and assigns, upon the confirmation of the sale and upon payment to him by _______________________ of the purchase price.

Witness my hand and official seal, this __________ day of ____________, _______.

_______________________________ (SEAL)

[Mayor of the City of _______________________]

[Chair of the Board of Commissioners

of _______________________ County]

Attested by:

____

(Seal)   Clerk to the Board

NORTH CAROLINA

_______________________ COUNTY

I, _______________________, Notary Public for said County and State, certify that _______________________ personally appeared before me this day, (attesting officer) and being by me duly sworn, acknowledged that he or she is clerk to the board of _______________________ [County] [a municipal corporation] and that by authority duly given and as the act of the [county] [municipality], the foregoing instrument was signed in its name by the [mayor] [chair of the board of commissioners], sealed with its official seal, and attested by himself or herself as clerk to the board.

Witness my hand and official seal, this _____ day of _______________________, _______.

Seal

____

Notary Public

My commission expires _______________________, _______.

CONFIRMATION

G.S. 105-374(p) provides: "At any time after the expiration of ten days from the time the commissioner files his report, if no exception or increased bid has been filed, the commissioner may apply for judgment of confirmation; and in like manner he may apply for such a judgment after the court has passed upon any exceptions filed, or after any necessary resales have been held and reported and ten days have elapsed." This statutory provision must be read together with the provision of G.S. 1-339.25(a) regarding when the rights of the parties to the foreclosure become fixed: "If an upset bid or a motion for resale under G.S. 1-339.27A is not filed within 10 days following a sale, resale, or prior upset bid, the rights of the parties to the sale or resale become fixed." After the expiration of the ten-day period specified in G.S. 1-339.25(a), a motion by the commissioner for confirmation of the sale (Form 44) is appropriate.

The statute does not require the motion for confirmation to contain a statement that the commissioner is of the opinion that the price bid is fair and reasonable. Since bids at tax foreclosure sales may be below the true market value of the property [see, for example, City of Durham v. Keen, 40 N.C. App. 652 (1979)], the Machinery Act prudently does not require a commissioner in such a proceeding to make any statement as to the reasonableness of the bid in seeking confirmation. The act does provide that the court of its own motion may reject a bid and order a resale. It would seem that if the court, in exercising its discretion, rejects a bid for inadequacy and orders a resale and the property brings no increase on resale, the court should then have no difficulty in confirming the sale. If a better price is obtained by the resale, no one (except perhaps the initial bidder) is hurt.

The taxing unit may, of course, protect itself by entering a bid that is at least the amount of its tax claim, plus costs, at all sales. If the taxing unit intends to do this, then the tax collector or some other official of the unit must be present at the sale and actually enter a bid; the property is not automatically sold to the taxing unit by default. Nothing in the law requires the taxing unit to start the bidding at an amount sufficient to cover taxes and costs, and the provisions of G.S. 105-374(q) contemplate that in some cases property will be sold for less than that amount. If the bids made by private bidders are less than the amount necessary to cover taxes and costs, officials of the taxing unit must decide whether—considering the market value of the property and other circumstances—it makes more sense for the taxing unit to accept an inadequate bid and take a loss on some of the taxes and costs or to enter

FORM 44. MOTION FOR CONFIRMATION

STATE OF NORTH CAROLINA

COUNTY OF _______________________

File # _________________________________

In the General Court of Justice

_______________________ Court Division

____

Before the Clerk

Plaintiff

vs.   MOTION TO CONFIRM

____

Defendant(s)

To the _______________________ of the _______________________ Court of

_______________________ County:

    Now comes the undersigned commissioner and reports:

    That more than ten days have elapsed since the sale of the real property described in the judgment in this action [or since the last upset bid] and since the report of the sale to the court, and that no advanced or upset bid [or no further upset bid or motion for resale] has been offered for the real property.

    Wherefore the undersigned commissioner moves that the court confirm the sale and direct him or her to execute a deed for the property, upon payment of the purchase price, and to disburse the money in the proper manner and report to the court such disbursements.

    Respectfully submitted, this __________ day of _______________________, _______.

____

Commissioner

a bid for the minimum amount necessary, purchase the property, and then later try to resell the property to a private purchaser. (Chapter 3 discusses the options available to a taxing unit that purchases property at a foreclosure sale.)

JUDGMENT OF CONFIRMATION

G.S. 105-374(p) provides that the judgment of confirmation (Form 45) shall direct the commissioner to deliver the deed on payment of the purchase price. The amounts of the attorney's and commissioner's fees should be included in the judgment. The judgment of confirmation "may be rendered by the Clerk of the Superior Court, subject to appeal in the same manner as appeals are taken from other judgments of said clerk."

FORM 45. JUDGMENT OF CONFIRMATION

STATE OF NORTH CAROLINA

COUNTY OF _______________________

File # _______________________

In the General Court of Justice

_______________________ Court Division

Before the Clerk

____

Plaintiff

vs.

JUDGMENT

____

Defendant(s)

This matter was heard before the undersigned clerk of the superior court upon the report of _______________________, Commissioner, filed on the __________ day of _______________________, _______, and it appearing from the report that the commissioner did, on the __________ day of _______________________, _______, offer for sale the real property described in the judgment in this action, after due advertisement in accordance with law, at which sale _______________________ became the last and highest bidder for the amount of $__________; and it further appearing that the sale was regularly and lawfully conducted and that more than ten days have elapsed since the report of the sale was filed and no increased bids or exceptions have been filed with respect thereto [or, that the sale was regularly and lawfully conducted and that _______________________ offered the last upset bid in the amount of $_________, and that more than ten days have elapsed since the last upset bid, motion for resale, or resale];

It is therefore ordered that the sale be confirmed, and the commissioner is hereby ordered to deliver to the purchaser a deed to the real property in fee simple, upon receipt of the purchase price; that the attorney for the plaintiff is hereby allowed $__________ as an attorney fee, and this fee shall be taxed as part of the costs; it is further ordered that the commissioner appointed in this cause shall be allowed $__________ as a fee for his or her services rendered in connection herewith, and this fee shall also be taxed as part of the costs; and the commissioner is ordered to file his final report showing the disbursement of the proceeds of the sale in accordance with the judgment heretofore rendered in this action.

This __________ day of _______________________, _______.

____

Clerk of the Superior Court

COMMISSIONER'S DEED

Upon confirmation of the sale by the court, the commissioner should execute for the purchaser a deed conveying to him or her a fee simple estate in the property. G.S. 105-374(k) provides that the property is to be sold in "fee simple, free and clear of all interests, rights, claims and liens whatever"; the deed is not a general warranty deed. Including the file number of the action in the deed serves as a helpful reference. Form 46 should suffice.

The commissioner should execute and deliver the deed as soon after the confirmation as possible. Occasionally, when the taxing unit is the successful bidder at the foreclosure sale, there is a long delay between

FORM 46. COMMISSIONER'S DEED

STATE OF NORTH CAROLINA   COMMISSIONER'S DEED
COUNTY OF _________________________

    This deed, made this ________ day of _________________________________, _______, by
_________________________________, Commissioner, to _________________________________ of
_________________________________ County, North Carolina,

WITNESSETH

    That whereas _________________________ was appointed commissioner under an order of
the _________________________ Court of _________________________ County,
North Carolina, in the tax foreclosure proceeding entitled "_________________________ vs.
_________________________" [File #___________]; and _________________________
was directed by the order as commissioner to sell the property hereinafter described at public sale
after due advertisement according to law; and

    Whereas _________________________, commissioner, did on the _________ day of
_________________________, _______, offer the land hereinafter described at a public sale at
the ____ County Courthouse door,
in _________________________, and _________________________ became the last and
highest bidder for said land for the sum of $__________; and the sale having been confirmed,
and _________________________, commissioner, having been ordered to execute a deed to the
purchaser upon payment of the purchase money;

FORM 46. COMMISSIONER'S DEED

Now, in consideration of the premises and the sum of $_________, receipt of which is hereby acknowledged, __________________________, commissioner, does, by these presents, hereby bargain, sell, grant, and convey to _____________________________, and ___________________________ successors, heirs and assigns, that property situated in __________________________ County, North Carolina, and described as follows:

[copy full legal description as it appears
in the complaint and judgment].

This conveyance is made subject to ______ county and city property taxes, the payment of which shall be assumed by the purchaser. To have and to hold the aforesaid tract of land, to __________________________ and __________________________ successors, heirs and assigns forever, in as full and ample manner as __________________________, commissioner, is authorized and empowered to convey the same.

In witness whereof, __________________________, commissioner, has hereunto set his or her hand and seal.

(SEAL)

____
Commissioner

NORTH CAROLINA

___________ COUNTY

I, ____ of this county, do hereby certify that ___________________________________, commissioner, grantor, personally appeared before me this day and acknowledged the execution of the foregoing deed.

Witness my hand and official seal this _________ day of ___________________,

______.

____
Notary Public

My commission expires __________________________

confirmation and execution of the deed, and sometimes the need for execution is overlooked entirely. This is troublesome when the taxing unit later attempts to sell the property to a private purchaser and the attorney for the purchaser finds no deed of record to the taxing unit.

COMMISSIONER'S FINAL REPORT

G.S. 105-374(q) requires the commissioner who makes the sale to file a full report to the court within five days after delivery of the deed. This report (Form 47) must show delivery of the deed, receipt of the purchase price, and disbursement of the proceeds, accompanied by receipts evidencing all disbursements. The statute also provides for the order of distribution of the proceeds of the sale as follows:

1. First, to payment of all costs of the action, including the commissioner's fee and attorney's fee, which costs shall be paid to the officials or funds entitled thereto;

2. Then to the payment of taxes, penalties and interest for which the real property was ordered to be sold, and in case the funds remaining are insufficient for this purpose, they shall be distributed pro rata to the various taxing units for whose taxes the property was ordered sold;

3. Then pro rata to the payment of any special benefit assessments for which the property was ordered sold, together with interest and costs thereon;

4. Then pro rata to payment of taxes, penalties, interest and costs of taxing units that were parties to the foreclosure action but which filed no answers therein;

5. Then pro rata to payment of special benefit assessments of taxing units that were parties to the foreclosure action but which filed no answers therein, together with interest and costs thereon;

6. And any balance then remaining shall be paid in accordance with any directions given by the court and, in the absence of such directions, shall be paid into court for the benefit of the persons entitled thereto.

G.S. 105-376(b) provides that if a taxing unit becomes the purchaser at a foreclosure sale, it may, "in the discretion of its governing body, pay only that part of the purchase price that would not be distributed to it and other taxing units on account of taxes, interest, penalties and such costs as accrued prior to the initiation of the foreclosure action. . . . Thereafter, in such a case, the purchasing taxing unit shall hold the property for the benefit of all taxing units that have an interest in the property as defined in this subsection (b)."[20] The purchasing taxing unit may withhold the payment of taxes to itself and to other taxing units, but in that event it will hold the property as trustee for the other taxing units as well as for itself. The income from the property, or the proceeds of any subsequent sale thereof, will have

---

20. N.C. Gen. Stat. § 105-376(b) specifies how the interest of each taxing unit is to be determined.

FORM 47. COMMISSIONER'S FINAL REPORT

STATE OF NORTH CAROLINA

COUNTY OF _______________________

File # ___________________________

In the General Court of Justice

______________________ Court Division

Before the Clerk

____

Plaintiff

vs.

REPORT

____

Defendant(s)

To the Honorable ______________________________, the Clerk of the Superior Court:

The undersigned, _____________________________, commissioner, respectfully reports to the court:

That he or she has executed and delivered to the purchaser of the real property described in the judgment a deed therefor as ordered by the court and has received the purchase price for the property; and the commissioner reports receipts and disbursements as follows:

Receipts

Date ______________

__________________________ received of _________________________ purchase price $_____________.

Disbursements

[Set out every item of disbursement in the order listed in G.S. 105-374(q) so that the purchase price will be fully accounted for. Each item should be supported by a receipt.]

Respectfully submitted, this ___________ day of _______________________, ________.

____

Commissioner

Sworn to and subscribed before me this ________ day of ______________, ______.

Audited and approved by: ____

_______________ of Superior Court

Date: ______________________________

to be distributed among the taxing units in proportion to their interests. (These matters are discussed in detail in Chapter 3.)

MEMORANDUM TO TAX OFFICES

After the attorney has filed a final report with the court, it is very helpful to the tax assessor and collector if he or she sends them a memorandum regarding the foreclosure and sale. The memorandum should state the name of the former owner of the property, the tax map block and lot description, the date of the sale, and the name and address of the new owner.

2

FORMS AND PROCEDURES FOR AN *IN REM* FORECLOSURE UNDER G.S. 105-375

FORMS AND PROCEDURES FOR AN *IN REM* FORECLOSURE UNDER G.S. 105-375

INTRODUCTION

An alternative method of foreclosure to the mortgage type is available to taxing units under G.S. 105-375. This is the *in rem* method, a relatively simple and inexpensive means of foreclosing the tax lien and selling the property, thereby returning the property to the active tax rolls. The legal theory underlying *in rem* foreclosure is that the land itself— the *res*—is being proceeded against, rather than the landowner. On this theory the summary notice procedures are justified.

There are two prerequisites to the use of the *in rem* procedure: the taxing unit must have advertised its tax liens as required by G.S. 105-369, and the governing board of the taxing unit must direct the tax collector to file tax judgments, thereby beginning the *in rem* foreclosure. Judgments may be docketed no earlier than thirty days after the lien advertisement. The tax collector must send notices of the docketing to the listing owner, to the current owner of the property if different from the listing owner, and to lienholders of record. This includes any person who holds a lien of record against the listing owner and any subsequent owner or owners, including the current owner; and it includes liens referred to in an instrument of conveyance from the listing owner or subsequent owners (conveyances in which a lien is assumed or in which property is received subject to a lien).

After the judgment has been docketed for three months, execution may be issued on it and the property sold under execution. Before the property is sold, notice by registered or certified mail must be sent to the listing owner and to the current owner if different from the listing owner.

With the addition of appropriate allegations, the *in rem* procedure can be used to foreclose the liens of special assessments.

This chapter's scope does not include defending or attacking the constitutional validity of the *in rem* method of foreclosure. The decision in *Henderson County v. Osteen,*[1] however, strongly supports the position that *in rem* foreclosures are constitutional if conducted strictly in accordance with the statute. The lesson of that case and its sequel[2] is that every required step called for by G.S. 105-375 must be taken and documented. A record of every step should be made, and copies of all significant documents should be placed in the tax collector's file.

Although an *in rem* foreclosure can be undertaken by the tax collector, with assistance as needed from the taxing unit's attorney, the staff member who prepares and files the foreclosure documents should be trained in title searching and should be meticulous in following and documenting the required procedures. The 1989 amendments to G.S. 105-375(c) that require notice to be given to all lienholders of record, including those who hold liens against grantees of the listing owner and their successors, make essential a search of the records in the offices of the register of deeds and clerk of superior court so that a chain of title can be constructed and the lienholders identified. This requires that the person handling the foreclosure be familiar with the indexes and records in those offices. Several court cases, including the *Osteen* cases discussed above, demonstrate that there is very little margin for error in the *in rem* procedure. Unless every *t* is crossed and every *i* dotted, courts are inclined to sustain a challenge to the procedure.

FORECLOSURE HISTORY

To help accomplish all of the steps in proper sequence, a checklist like Form 1 should be placed in the front of each *in rem* foreclosure file and used. The form shown is, with a few modifications, the one developed by Alamance County, a taxing unit that has successfully used the *in rem* method for several years.

---

1. 292 N.C. 692, 235 S.E.2d 166 (1977), discussed in W. Campbell, In Rem *Foreclosures: Henderson County v. Osteen*, PROPERTY TAX BULLETIN 48 (Institute of Government, August 29, 1977). *See also* W. Campbell and V. Soto, *The Constitutionality of* In Rem *Tax Lien Foreclosures: Recent Cases*, PROPERTY TAX BULLETIN 54 (Institute of Government, 1980); W. Campbell, In Rem *Foreclosures: The U.S. Supreme Court Imposes Additional Notice Requirements*, PROPERTY TAX BULLETIN 62 (Institute of Government, 1983); and W. CAMPBELL AND L. HAGIN, SPECIAL SERIES No. 6: A REVIEW OF THE CONSTITUTIONALITY OF *IN REM* TAX FORECLOSURES (Institute of Government, 1991).

2. Henderson County v. Osteen, 297 N.C. 113, 254 S.E.2d 160 (1979).

FORM 1. OFFICE OF TAX COLLECTOR FORECLOSURE HISTORY

Name _______________________________ Tax Map No. ___________ Date _____________
       [Listing owner]

☐   Tax lien advertisement date ______________________________
☐ * Letter to taxpayer (two weeks after tax lien advertisement)

      ____

☐   Title search _______________________________
☐ * Letter to deed-of-trust holder_______________________________
☐   Certified letters to taxpayer, current owner, and lienholders (thirty days before judgment)

      ____

☐   Advertisement for nonreceipt (once a week for two weeks beginning ten days
      after nonreceipt) ______________________________
☐   Docketing of judgment (no earlier than thirty days after tax lien advertisement)

      ____

☐ * Personal contact attempt (two months after judgment)

      ____

☐ * Letter informing of execution (two months after judgment)

      ____

☐   Request for execution (no earlier than three months after judgment)

      ____

☐   Sheriff's delivery of execution ______________________________
☐   Certified letter informing listing owner and current owner of sale (thirty days before sale)

      ____

☐   Two weeks of advertisements ______________________________
☐   Post notice of sale for 20 days preceding sale ______________________________
☐ * For-sale sign placed on property ______________________________
☐   Sale held ______________________________
☐   Report of sale ______________________________
☐   Order to execute deed ______________________________
☐   Execution and delivery of deed ______________________________

     * These items are not required by statute but may help either in getting the taxes paid before the property is sold under execution or in giving every possible notice to the taxpayer and others interested in the property.

LETTER TO LISTING TAXPAYER, CURRENT OWNER, AND LIENHOLDERS

The theory of foreclosure under G.S. 105-375 is that the land itself is liable for the taxes, that those who have an interest in it have no personal liability for the taxes, and that as a result those who have an interest in the land—the *res*—have a duty to be alert to the possibility of foreclosure. Thus personal notice to those who have an interest in the property is not essential; the action is *in rem*—that is, the foreclosure runs against the land itself, not against its owners. In such an action the tax collector certifies the fact of nonpayment of taxes, and the certificate is given the status of a judgment of the court.

Before the collector makes the certificate and dockets it as a judgment, G.S. 105-375(c) requires that a preliminary step be taken:

> The tax collector filing the certificate provided for in subsection (b), above, shall, at least 30 days prior to docketing the judgment, send a registered or certified letter, return receipt requested, to the listing taxpayer at his last known address, and to all lienholders of record who have a lien against the listing taxpayer or against any subsequent owner of the property (including any liens referred to in the conveyance of the property to the listing taxpayer or to the subsequent owner of the property), stating that the judgment will be docketed and that execution will be issued thereon in the manner provided by law. A notice stating that the judgment will be docketed and that execution will be issued thereon shall also be mailed by certified or registered mail, return receipt requested, to the current owner of the property (if different from the listing owner) if: (i) a deed or other instrument transferring title to and containing the name of the current owner was recorded in the office of the register of deeds or filed or docketed in the office of the clerk of superior court after January 1 of the first year in which the property was listed in the name of the listing owner, and (ii) the tax collector can obtain the current owner's mailing address through the exercise of due diligence.

To obtain the names and addresses of the persons to whom the letters of notification must be sent, the tax collector or the attorney for the taxing unit must search the register of deeds' and clerk of superior court's records. The collector can obtain the name of the listing owner for the tax year or years in question from the tax assessor. The correctness of the name and the listing information and address should always be verified by examining the title document by which the listing owner acquired the property. For example, the tax listing may be in the name of a man, but the deed may show that the grantees are a husband and wife who own the land as tenants by entireties. In this case, two separate letters would have to be mailed, one to the husband and one to the wife. Also, an examination of the deed, will, or other title document may show that the tax assessor has been using the wrong address and all of the tax bills have therefore been sent to the wrong address.

To search the records for the name of the current owner, the tax collector must first determine from the abstracts or other records in the tax assessor's office the year in which the property involved in the foreclosure was first listed in the name of the listing owner. Then, beginning with January 1 of that year, the collector must examine the grantor-grantee real property indexes in the register of deeds' office to see whether the listing owner has deeded the property to another person and the Index to Estates in the clerk of superior court's office to see whether the property has passed to a new owner by will or intestate succession. The collector should also check the Index to Judgments, Liens, and Lis Pendens in the clerk's office to determine whether title to the property has been transferred by judgment; although most judgments transferring title to real property are recorded in the register of deeds' office (G.S. 1-228 provides for the registration of such judgments), some may not be, and an examination of this index will reveal those.

"Due diligence" in finding the current owner's mailing address requires the collector to use the name found on any recorded instruments—together with any other available information concerning the address—and then, at a minimum, to search for that person's address in local telephone directories, city directories, voter registration lists, and the tax scroll.

To find the names and addresses of lienholders of record, the tax collector should examine the appropriate indexes in the register of deeds' and the clerk of superior court's offices in the names of the listing owner, the current owner, and any intermediate owners for the presence of any liens recorded against them. For the sake of comprehensiveness, the collector should also examine the indexes in the names of any owners preceding the listing owner, if necessary to extend the search to a period of thirty years before the date on which the judgment was docketed.

A few points concerning the mailing of the notices deserve emphasis:

1. The letters must be sent to the listing taxpayer at his last known address and to the current owner at his address by registered or certified mail, return receipt requested. To be certain that proper notice is given, many collectors advise that

FORM 2. LETTER TO LISTING TAXPAYER

Dear _______________________________:

This is to advise you that taxes assessed against the property described below and listed in your name for the years _______________ are past due and remain unpaid. These taxes, together with penalties, interest, and costs, constitute a first lien upon the real estate described below. Take notice that unless the amount shown below is paid to me within thirty days from this date, or a satisfactory arrangement for payment is made, it will be my duty to docket a judgment against the property in the Office of the Clerk of the Superior Court of _______________________________ County. The judgment will be executed in the manner provided by law, and the property will be sold at public sale to the highest bidder.

Amount of tax	$ ______________________
Penalties and interest	$ ______________________
Costs	$ ______________________
Total due	$ ______________________

Property: [enter here a description sufficient to identify the property].

If the judgment is docketed or execution is placed in the hands of the sheriff, additional costs will accrue. I trust that you will pay the amount due promptly and avoid either added expense to you or the loss of your property.

Very truly yours,

____
Tax Collector

the post office be asked to send these letters marked "deliver to addressee only."

2. The letters should be sent at least thirty days before the judgment is docketed.

3. Because it may become necessary to prove that the letters were mailed, a copy of each letter with the postal receipts attached showing that the letter was sent by registered or certified mail should be kept in the file.

4. If the property subject to foreclosure is held as an estate by the entireties, the foreclosure action must be directed against both husband and wife, and all required notices must be

FORM 3. LETTER TO CURRENT OWNER

Dear _______________________________:

The records of _______________________________ County show that you are the owner of the real property described below. In the year _________, the property was listed in the name of _______________________________. Taxes assessed against the property for that year are past due and remain unpaid. These taxes, together with penalties, interest, and costs, constitute a first lien upon the property. Take notice that unless the amount shown below is paid to me within thirty days from this date, or a satisfactory arrangement for payment is made, it will be my duty to docket a judgment against the property in the Office of the Clerk of Superior Court of _______________________ County. The judgment will be executed in the manner provided by law, and the property will be sold at public sale to the highest bidder.

Amount of tax	$ _______________________
Penalties and interest	$ _______________________
Costs	$ _______________________
Total due	$ _______________________

Property: [enter here a description sufficient to identify the property].

If the judgment is docketed or execution is placed in the hands of the sheriff, additional costs will accrue. I trust that you will pay the amount due promptly and avoid either added expense to you or the loss of your property.

Very truly yours,

____
Tax Collector

sent to both. To be safe, separate certified or registered letters should be sent to each spouse. This is required even though the property may have been listed in the husband's name alone [see Edwards v. Arnold, 250 N.C. 500, 109 S.E.2d 205 (1959)].

Form 2 is for the letter to the listing owner, Form 3 is for the letter to the current owner, and Form 4 is for the letter to lienholders.

FORM 4. LETTER TO LIENHOLDERS

Dear _________________________:

The records of _____________________________ County show that you have a lien against the property described below. In the year _________, the property was listed in the name of _________________________________. Taxes assessed against the property for that year are past due and remain unpaid. These taxes, together with penalties, interest, and costs, constitute a first lien upon the property. Take notice that unless the amount shown below is paid to me within thirty days from this date, or a satisfactory arrangement for payment is made, it will be my duty to docket a judgment against the property in the Office of the Clerk of Superior Court of _________________ County. The judgment will be executed in the manner provided by law, and the property will be sold at public sale to the highest bidder. If the property is sold, it will be sold free and clear of your lien.

Amount of tax	$ _____________________
Penalties and interest	$ _____________________
Costs	$ _____________________
Total due	$ _____________________

Property: [enter here a description sufficient to identify the property].

If the judgment is docketed or execution is placed in the hands of the sheriff, additional costs will accrue. I trust that you will pay the amount due promptly and avoid either added expense to you or the loss of your lien on the property.

Very truly yours,

____
Tax Collector

NEWSPAPER NOTICE OF THE DOCKETING OF THE JUDGMENT

G.S. 105-375(c) provides that if the tax collector has not received return receipts indicating that the letters of notice were received by the taxpayer, current owner, and lienholders within ten days after the letters were mailed, he or she must publish a notice of the docketing of the judgment in a newspaper having a general circulation in the county. The notice must be published once a week for two consecutive weeks. It must name the listing taxpayer, the current owner, and the unnotified lienholders; briefly describe the property; give the date of the proposed docketing of

FORM 5. NEWSPAPER NOTICE OF THE DOCKETING
OF THE JUDGMENT

STATE OF NORTH CAROLINA

COUNTY OF _______________________

File # ________________________________

In the General Court of Justice

________________________ Court Division

____

Plaintiff

vs.

NOTICE

____

Defendant(s)

Pursuant to the requirements of G.S. 105-375(c), notice is hereby given to

_______________________   (listing taxpayer)

_______________________   (current owner)

____

_______________________   (lienholders)

____

that a judgment of foreclosure will be docketed against the property described below on _______________________, ________.

[Here enter a brief description of the property.]

Execution will be issued on the judgment, and the property will be sold as provided by law. The tax lien, including interests and costs, may be paid before the judgment is docketed and at any time thereafter as allowed by law.

____

(Dates notice is to be run
in newspaper)

____

Tax Collector

____

Date notice prepared

the judgment; state that execution will issue thereon as provided by law; and state that the lien may be paid before the judgment is entered. This notice must be published if the letter was not received by the listing owner, or the current owner, *or* any lienholder. Form 5 is for the newspaper notice of docketing. Form 6 is for the publisher's affidavit that the notice was in fact published.

JUDGMENT FOR TAXES

G.S. 105-375(b) provides that under the circumstances outlined in the introduction to these forms, the tax collector is to file "with the clerk of superior court a certificate showing the following: the name of the taxpayer listing real property on which the taxes are a lien, together with the amount of taxes, penalties, interest and costs that are a lien thereon; the year or years for which the taxes are due; and a description of the property sufficient to permit its identification by parol testimony."[3]

The certificate-judgment should be indexed in the Index to Judgments, Liens, and Lis Pendens in the name of the listing taxpayer. The clerk is only required to docket and index the judgment; he or she is not required to open a case file. G.S. 7A-308(a)(11) provides that the clerk's fee for docketing and indexing the judgment is $6.00 for the first page and $0.25 for each additional page. Although G.S. 105-375(b) provides that this fee is to be collected when the taxes are paid or the property is sold, the clerk may insist that G.S. 7A-308(b) requires it to be paid before the judgment is docketed. If this occurs, the collector should pay the fee and add it to the costs to be collected when the taxes are paid or the property is sold.

G.S. 105-375(c) provides that all costs of mailing and publication, plus an administrative charge of $50.00, shall be added to the taxes as part of the judgment.

G.S. 105-375(d) then characterizes the effect of docketing and indexing this certificate:

> Immediately upon the docketing and indexing of a certificate as provided in subdivision (b), above, the taxes, penalties, interest and costs shall constitute a valid judgment against the real property described therein, with the priority provided for tax liens in § 105-356. The judgment, except as expressly provided in this section, shall have the same force and effect as a duly rendered judgment of the superior court directing sale of the property for the satisfaction of the tax lien, and shall bear interest at the rate of eight percent (8%) per annum.

3. "By agreement between the governing bodies, two or more taxing units may consolidate their liens for purposes of docketing a judgment." N.C. GEN. STAT. § 105-375(k).

FORM **6.** PUBLISHER'S AFFIDAVIT

STATE OF NORTH CAROLINA
COUNTY OF _______________________

File # _________________________________

In the General Court of Justice

_________________________________ Court Division

____
Plaintiff

vs.   AFFIDAVIT

____
Defendant(s)

_________________________________, being sworn, says:

That he or she is the ____* of
the _________________________________ Company engaged in publishing a newspaper known as
_________________________________, published, issued, and entered as second-class mail in the City of
_________________________________, in said county and state;

That he or she is authorized to make this affidavit and sworn statement;

That the notice, a true copy of which is attached hereto, was published in the newspaper on
the following dates: _________________________; and that the newspaper in which such notice
was published was, at the time of each and every such publication, a newspaper meeting all of the
requirements and qualifications of Section 1-597 of the General Statutes.

This ____________ day of _________________________________, ________.

____
Affiant

Sworn to and subscribed before me this ______________ day of _________________, ________.

____
Notary Public
My commission expires _________________________________.

____

*Insert here the proper designation of affiant's position with the newspaper, such as owner, publisher, editor, managing editor, or business manager. (See G.S. 1-600 for officials authorized to make affidavit of publication.)

Note that interest on the taxes stops on the date the judgment is docketed. From that date, 8 percent interest runs against the total amount of the judgment, which is the sum of the taxes, interest, mailing and advertising costs, and $50.00 administrative charge.

Form 7 is designed to serve as the collector's certificate, which, when docketed and indexed as outlined here, becomes a judgment. Although the statute merely requires a description of the property "sufficient to permit its identification by parol testimony," the full legal description taken from the last recorded deed should probably be used, together with a reference to that deed.

EXECUTION

Often the property owner or some other interested party will want to pay the taxes after the judgment has been docketed and before execution is issued and the property is actually sold. G.S. 105-375(g) deals with this situation: "Upon payment in full of any judgment docketed under this section, together with interest thereon and costs accrued to the date of payment, the tax collector receiving payment shall certify the fact thereof to the clerk of superior court and cancel the judgment."

Furthermore, G.S. 105-375(f) provides a means for moving to set aside the judgment: "At any time prior to the issuance of execution, any person having an interest in the real property to be foreclosed may appear before the clerk of superior court and move to set aside the judgment on the ground that the tax has been paid or that the tax lien on which the judgment is based is invalid." In some cases, the taxpayer, or someone on behalf of the taxpayer, may wish to make a partial payment on the judgment. G.S. 1-239 allows this, and the clerk will make an entry on the judgment showing the amount of the payment.

In most cases, however, the taxing unit, through its collector, will have execution issued on its judgment. G.S. 105-375(i) outlines the steps: "At any time after three months and before two years from the indexing of the judgment as provided in subdivision (b), above, execution shall be issued at the request of the tax collector in the same manner as executions are issued upon other judgments of the superior court. . . ."[4] G.S. 7A-308(a)(5) provides that the clerk's fee for issuing the execution is $22.50.

It should be pointed out that G.S. 105-375(k) states that "one execution may issue for separate judgments in favor of one or more taxing units against the same property for different years' taxes." Once issued,

---

4. "By agreement between the governing bodies, two or more taxing units . . . may have one execution issued for separate judgments, against the same property." *Id.*

FORM 7. JUDGMENT FOR TAXES

STATE OF NORTH CAROLINA

COUNTY OF ________________________

File # ___________________________________

In the General Court of Justice

_________________________________ Court Division

Before the Clerk

____

Plaintiff

vs.

JUDGMENT FOR TAXES

____

Defendant(s)

[name of listing taxpayer]

Pursuant to the provisions of Section 105-375 of the General Statutes, I hereby certify that taxes duly levied and assessed against the property described below and listed in the name of ____________________, by ____________________ County [City, Town] for the year __________ are due and unpaid; that these taxes constitute a first lien upon the real property hereinafter described prior to any other lien that is or may become attached to the real property; that the amount now owing to ____________________ County [City, Town] on account of the taxes, penalties, interest, and costs is as follows:

Amount of tax for ________	$______________
Penalties	$______________
Costs of advertising	$______________
Subtotal	$______________
Interest on the subtotal	
from ____________ to date	$______________
Administrative charge	$______50.00___
Mailing and publication costs	$______________
Total amount of judgment	$______________

That ______________________________ County [City, Town] has a first lien for the amount of the judgment, plus interest at the rate of 8 percent per annum from date until paid, upon the following described real estate located in ____________________ Township, ____________________ County, North Carolina:

[insert full legal description and deed reference].

This __________ day of______________________________, ________ .

____

Tax Collector for [City] [Town]

[County] of ______________________________

Filed ______________________________

Docketed ______________, at ________ ____.M.

____

Clerk of the Superior Court

an execution is valid for only ninety days (G.S. 1-339.48), and the first notice of sale must be published within ninety days of the date the execution was issued.

Form 8 is for the request for execution by the tax collector. Form 9 is for the execution itself.

NOTICE OF SALE UNDER EXECUTION

G.S. 105-375(i) states that when execution has been issued on the tax judgment, "the real property shall be sold by the sheriff in the same manner as other real property is sold under execution" with two exceptions, to be pointed out in notes to the appropriate forms. In general, then, the sale will be conducted under the provisions of G.S. Chapter 1, Article 29B.

However, a significant modification of usual procedures appears in G.S. 105-375(i)(4):

> In any advertisement or posted notice of sale under execution, the sheriff may (and at the request of the governing body of the taxing unit shall) combine the advertisements or notices for properties to be sold under executions against the properties of different taxpayers in favor of the same taxing unit or group of units; however, the property included in each judgment shall be separately described and the name of the listing taxpayer specified in connection with each.

Form 10, for notice of sale under execution, is drawn to meet the general legal requirements, but it is also drawn as a combined notice of the kind envisioned by G.S. 105-375(i). (A county bringing the foreclosure may find it useful to group the parcels in each township together on the form.) As required by statute, the name of the listing taxpayer is shown in connection with each parcel, and, as an aid to bidders at the sale, the amount due is also shown in connection with each parcel.

Note, too, that the first exception set out in G.S. 105-375(i) to the usual execution procedure specifically provides that when execution is issued, no debtor's exemption is to be allowed. Such an exception is authorized by Article X, Section 2, of the North Carolina Constitution.

As required by G.S. 1-339.52, the notice of sale must be posted in the area designated by the clerk of superior court for the posting of notices for at least twenty days immediately preceding the sale, and it must be published in a newspaper qualified for legal advertising in the county at least once a week for two successive weeks before the sale. The period between the first and last dates on which the notice is published, both

FORM **8.** REQUEST FOR EXECUTION

STATE OF NORTH CAROLINA

COUNTY OF ______________________

File # ________________________________

In the General Court of Justice

Superior Court Division

Before the Clerk

____

Plaintiff

vs.

REQUEST FOR EXECUTION

____

Defendant(s)

To the Clerk of the Superior Court of ________________________________ County:

Whereas there is docketed in the Office of the Clerk of the Superior Court of ________________ County a judgment in favor of the above-named plaintiff and against real property listed for taxes by the above-named defendant in the amount of $______________, with interest on this judgment at 8 percent per annum from ______________, ________, all amounting to $______________ as of this date, which judgment constitutes a first lien prior to all other liens upon the property located in ________________ Township, ______________ County, North Carolina, and described as follows:

[insert full legal description].

And whereas the judgment remains unpaid and the amount now actually due thereon, including principal, interest, and costs, is $______________, and more than three months have elapsed since the judgment was filed in this court;

Therefore, pursuant to the authority vested in me by G.S. 105-375(i), I hereby request that execution upon the judgment be issued and that the liens upon the above-described property be foreclosed and the property be sold as provided by law.

This ___________ day of ________________________________, ________.

____

Tax Collector of ________________________________

[City] [County]

dates inclusive, shall not be less than seven days, including Sundays, and the date of the last publication shall be not more than ten days preceding the date of the sale.

FORM 9. EXECUTION

STATE OF NORTH CAROLINA

COUNTY OF ___________________________

File # ___________________________________

In the General Court of Justice

Superior Court Division

Before the Clerk

____

Plaintiff

vs.

EXECUTION

____

Defendant(s)

To the Sheriff of _______________________________ County:

Whereas there is docketed in the Office of the Clerk of the Superior Court of _______________________ County a judgment in favor of the above-named plaintiff and against real property listed for taxes by the above-named defendant in the amount of $__________________, with interest on this judgment at 8 percent per annum from _________________, _______, all amounting to $__________ as of this date, which judgment constitutes a first lien prior to all other liens upon the property located in _______________________ Township, ___________________ County, North Carolina, and described as follows:

[insert full legal description].

And whereas the judgment remains unpaid and the amount now actually due thereon, including principal, interest, and costs, is $________;

You are, therefore, commanded to satisfy the judgment by a sale of the property or so much thereof as is necessary to pay the judgment, principal, interest, and costs as they may appear at the time of the final report, and to return this execution within not more than ninety days from the date hereof to the undersigned.

This execution is issued this __________ day of ____________________, ________.

____

Clerk of the Superior Court

RETURN ON EXECUTION

Received: _______________________________, ________.

Served: _______________________________, ________.

____,

Sheriff of

_______________________ County, North Carolina

By: _________________________________,

Deputy

FORM 10. NOTICE OF SALE UNDER EXECUTION

STATE OF NORTH CAROLINA

COUNTY OF _______________________

____

Plaintiff

vs.

____

Defendant(s)

File # _________________________________

In the General Court of Justice

Superior Court Division

Before the Clerk

NOTICE OF SALE OF LAND

UNDER EXECUTION

By virtue of certain executions directed to the undersigned from the Superior Court of _______________________ County in the actions entitled [insert name of plaintiff unit] vs. the several judgment debtors hereinafter set out, I will, on _______________________, _________, at 12:00 noon, at the _______________________ County courthouse door, in the city [town] of _______________________, sell to the highest bidder for cash to satisfy the executions the several parcels of real property separately described following the name of each judgment debtor hereinafter set out.

The executions were issued pursuant to judgment duly recorded in the office of the Clerk of the Superior Court for _______________________ County, and the executions are in the amounts specified in each case following the name of the judgment debtor and the description of the real estate, plus costs of sale, as follows:

The following described property is all located in _______________________ Township, _______________________ County, North Carolina:

1. The real property listed for taxes for the year _________ in the name of _______________________, the judgment debtor, and described as follows:

[insert full legal description].

Amount due under judgment, including costs: $_______________.

2. The real property listed for taxes for the year _________ in the name of _______________________, the judgment debtor, and described as follows:

[insert full legal description].

Amount due under judgment, including costs: $_______________.

[The form can be expanded here to take care of other judgments and other townships.]

The sale will be made subject to all outstanding taxes and all local improvement assessments against the above-described property not included in the judgment in the above-entitled cause.

This _________ day of _______________________, _________.

____

Sheriff of _______________________ County

If the tax collector's title examination has disclosed a federal tax lien on the property, Section 7425 of the Internal Revenue Code requires that notice of the sale be given to the local District Director of Internal Revenue at least twenty-five days before the sale. For copies of the form on which notice must be given and instructions for completing the form, write to:

> District Director of Internal Revenue
> 320 Federal Place
> Greensboro, NC 27401
> Attention: Chief, Special Procedures Staff

PUBLISHER'S AFFIDAVIT

Form 11 is for the publisher's affidavit that the notice was in fact published; this form is identical to Form 6 in this chapter.

FORM 11. PUBLISHER'S AFFIDAVIT (SEE FORM 6)

NOTICE OF SALE TO LISTING TAXPAYER AND CURRENT OWNER

The second exception set out in G.S. 105-375(i) to the usual procedure in sales under execution is: "In lieu of personal service of notice on the owner of the property, registered or certified mail notice shall be mailed to the listing owner (and to the current owner if notice was required to be mailed to him pursuant to subsection (c), above) at his last known address at least thirty days prior to the day fixed for the sale." The notice to be mailed is a copy of the notice of sale, which in executions other than tax foreclosures under G.S. 105-375 must be personally served on the judgment debtor (see G.S. 1-339.54). No letters need accompany the copies of the notices of sale. As with all other mailings in the *in rem* foreclosure, the tax collector should keep a record in the file that the notices were sent and also keep the return receipts.

This notice is expressly made in lieu of personal service. Nevertheless, in cases in which personal service has for some reason been obtained, the notice should still be mailed because the statute states that it "shall" be sent.

G.S. 105-375(i)(3) directs the sheriff to include the costs of mailing these notices in the amount of the judgment, but as a practical matter, this cannot be done. These costs should be added to the sheriff's fees and deducted from the purchase price.

PLACING A SIGN ON THE PROPERTY

In addition to sending the legally required notices of sale, several tax collectors using the *in rem* foreclosure have found it helpful to place a large sign on the property to be sold. As noted in chapter 1, the sign serves several purposes. It alerts adjacent property owners and other landowners in the neighborhood of the sale, and they are often good prospective bidders. It also, on occasion, turns up an heir or other person with a legal interest in the property, hitherto not to be found, who will pay the taxes before the property is sold.

A typical sign is:

<table>
<tr><td></td><td>TAX FORECLOSURE SALE OF THIS PROPERTY
to be held at 12:00 noon</td></tr>
<tr><td>date →</td><td>________________________________</td></tr>
<tr><td>county name →</td><td>at the _________________________ County Courthouse</td></tr>
<tr><td>tel. no of →
tax collector
or attorney</td><td>Call ___________________________
for further details</td></tr>
</table>

PAYMENT OF TAXES AND COSTS
AFTER EXECUTION IS ISSUED

Frequently, the property owner or someone acting on the property owner's behalf wishes to pay the taxes and costs after the execution has been issued and thereby stop the sale. This can be done, but several points should be noted about payment at this stage of the proceedings. First, payment should be made to the clerk of superior court so that he or she can properly indicate satisfaction of the judgment on the records and ensure that all fees and costs are paid. Second, if payment is tendered after the execution has been issued to the sheriff and the notices of sale have been mailed, G.S. 7A-311(a)(3) indicates that the sheriff must be paid the sale fees even though the property has not yet been sold. These fees are 5 percent of the first $500 and 2½ percent of all sums over

$500. Third, if payment is tendered after the property is sold, the judgment may be satisfied and the proceedings halted if the judgment and costs are paid, but G.S. 1-339.57 requires that this payment be made within the time allowed for any upset bid.

REPORT OF SALE

G.S. 1-339.63 requires the sheriff holding the sale to file a report of it with the clerk of superior court within five days of the sale. Form 12 is for that report.

Note that the clerk of superior court will usually require a separate report of sale for each property on which the liens are being foreclosed, even if sales of several different parcels are held at the same time.

UPSET BIDS

After the property has been sold, G.S. 1-339.64 provides for one or more upset bids. G.S. 1-339.64(a) sets forth the procedure as follows:

> (a)   An upset bid is an advanced, increased, or raised bid whereby a person offers to purchase real property theretofore sold for an amount exceeding the reported price or last upset bid by a minimum of five percent (5%) thereof, but in any event with a minimum increase of seven hundred fifty dollars ($750.00). Subject to the provisions of subsection (b) of this section, an upset bid shall be made by delivering to the clerk of superior court, with whom the report of sale or the last notice of upset bid was filed, a deposit in cash or by certified check or cashier's check satisfactory to the clerk in an amount greater than or equal to five percent (5%) of the amount of the upset bid but in no event less than seven hundred fifty dollars ($750.00). The deposit required by this section shall be filed with the clerk of the superior court, with whom the report of sale or the last notice of upset bid was filed, by the close of normal business hours on the tenth day after the filing of the report of sale or the last notice of upset bid and if the tenth day falls upon a Sunday or legal holiday or upon a day in which the office of the clerk is not open for the regular dispatch of its busness, the deposit may be made and the notice of upset bid may be filed on the day following when the office is open for the regular dispatch of its business. Except as provided in G.S. 1-339.66A and G.S. 1-339.69, there shall be no resales; however, there may be successive upset bids, each of which shall be followed by a period of 10 days for a further upset bid. If a timely motion for resale is filed under G.S. 1-339.66A, no upset bids may be

FORM 12. REPORT OF EXECUTION SALE

STATE OF NORTH CAROLINA File # _______________________

COUNTY OF _______________________ In the General Court of Justice

Superior Court Division

_______________________ Before the Clerk

Plaintiff

vs. REPORT OF EXECUTION SALE

____

Defendant(s)

Pursuant to the power and authority vested in me as sheriff under an execution issued in this cause by the Honorable _______________________, Clerk of the Superior Court of _______________________ County, on _______________________, _______, I offered for sale and sold at public auction for cash to the last and highest bidder the properties described in the execution, after due advertisement of the sale in the manner provided by the execution and prescribed by law, at _______________________, at _____ o'clock ___.M., on the ___________ day of _______________________, _______, to _______________________, the highest bidder, for $_____________.

This ___________ day of _______________________, _______,

____

Sheriff of _______________________ County

filed while the motion is pending. If an upset bid or a motion for resale under G.S. 1-339.66A is not filed within 10 days following a sale, resale, or prior upset bid, the rights of the parties to the sale or resale become fixed.

G.S. 1-339.64(e) requires a person making an upset bid to file a notice of upset bid with the clerk of superior court. The notice must:

1.   State the name, address, and telephone number of the upset bidder;
2.   Specify the amount of the upset bid;
3.   Provide that the sale shall remain open for a period of 10 days after the date on which the notice of upset bid is filed for the filing of additional upset bids as permitted by law; and
4.   Be signed by the upset bidder or the attorney or agent of the upset bidder.

FORM 13. ASSIGNMENT OF BID

STATE OF NORTH CAROLINA

COUNTY OF ______________________

____

Plaintiff

vs.

____

Defendant(s)

File # ________________________________

In the General Court of Justice
Superior Court Division
Before the Clerk

ASSIGNMENT

The [County] [City] of ______________________________ was the last and highest bidder for that certain tract or parcel of real property described in the execution in the above-entitled cause at a sale held on the ___________ day of ________________________________, _______, and I, ______________________________, as [Mayor of the city] [Chair of the Board of Commissioners of the county], pursuant to authority vested in me by resolution of the [City Council] [Board of County Commissioners] dated ______________________________, _______, do hereby, in consideration of ______________________________'s promise to pay the sum of $_____________, the amount of the bid, to the sheriff upon confirmation of the sale, sell, set over, transfer and assign the [county's] [city's] bid made at the sale unto ____, his or her heirs and assigns; and ____, sheriff in the sale, is hereby instructed to execute and deliver a deed conveying the real property to ______________________________, his or her heirs and assigns, upon the confirmation of the sale and upon payment to him or her by ______________________________ of the purchase price.

Witness my hand and seal, this ___________ day of ________________________, _______.

____
(Seal)
[Mayor of the City of ________________]
[Chair of the Board of Commissioners of
________________________ County]

Attested by: ______________________________
Clerk to the Board
(Seal)

NORTH CAROLINA

______________________________ County

I, ______________________________, Notary Public for said County and State, certify that ______________________________ personally appeared before me this day, and being by me duly sworn, acknowledged that he or she is clerk to the board of ______________________________ [County] [a municipal corporation] and that by authority duly given and as the act of the [county] [municipality], the foregoing instrument was signed in its name by the [mayor] [chair of the board of commissioners], sealed with its official seal, and attested by himself or herself as clerk to the board.

Witness my hand and seal, this ___________ day of ________________, _______.

(Seal)

____
Notary Public

My commission expires ______________________________, _______.

FORM 14. ORDER OF CONFIRMATION

STATE OF NORTH CAROLINA

COUNTY OF _______________________

File # _______________________________

In the General Court of Justice
Superior Court Division
Before the Clerk

____

Plaintiff

vs.

ORDER OF CONFIRMATION

____

Defendant(s)

     This matter was heard before the undersigned clerk of the superior court upon the report of ____, Sheriff of _________________ County, filed on the _______ day of _________________________, _______, and it appearing from the report that the sheriff did, on the _________ day of ____________, _______, offer for sale the real property described in the execution issued in this action, after due advertisement in accordance with law, at which sale _________________ became the last and highest bidder for the amount of $_________; and it further appearing that the sale was regularly and lawfully conducted and that more than ten days have elapsed since the report of the sale was filed and no increased bids or exceptions have been been filed with the respect thereto; or [that the sale was regularly and lawfully conducted and that ___________________ offered the last upset bid in the amount of $_________, and that more than ten days have elapsed since the last upset bid, motion for resale, or resale]; at which sale _____________________ became the last and highest bidder for the amount of $______________; and it further appearing that the sale was regularly and lawfully conducted and that more than ten days have elapsed since the report of the sale was filed and no increased bids or exceptions have been filed with respect thereto;[*]

     It is, therefore, ordered that the sale be confirmed, and the sheriff is hereby ordered to deliver to the purchaser[**] a deed to the real property in fee simple, upon receipt of the purchase price; and after deducting the expenses of the sale and fees allowed him or her by law, the sheriff is ordered to pay the proceeds of the sale to this court.

     This ___________ day of _______________________________, _______.

____
Clerk of the Superior Court

     * If the governing unit's bid has been assigned, add "and _________________, having been assigned the bid of the [City] [County] of ____________, by action of the [city council] [board of county commissioners] taken on, _____________, _______;"

     ** If there has been an assignment, substitute "assignee" for "purchaser."

FORM 15. SHERIFF'S DEED

STATE OF NORTH CAROLINA   SHERIFF'S DEED
COUNTY OF ______________________

    This deed, made this ___________ day of ______________________________, _________, by and between _______________________________, Sheriff of ________________________________ County, North Carolina, party of the first part, and _______________________________, party [parties] of the second part,

WITNESSETH

    That whereas the party of the first part, being duly authorized by an execution issued upon a certain judgment docketed in the office of the Clerk of the Superior Court for ____ County in a proceeding entitled " _________________________ vs. ____________________," (File #_________), and after due advertisement in accordance with law, did offer for sale and did sell, at public auction for cash to the highest bidder, at the courthouse door in ________________________________ County, on the ___________ day of _______________________________, real property herein described, when and where ________________________________ became the last and highest bidder for the same at the price of $_____________; and

    *Whereas ____ did, on _________________________________, _________, by proper resolution of the [Board of County Commissioners] [City Council] assign its bid to ___________________________________, party of the second part, for the sum of $_____________; and

    Whereas the sale has been confirmed by order of the superior court, and ________________________________, party of the second part, has fully paid the amount of the bid to the party of the first part;

    Now, therefore, in consideration of the premises and in further consideration of the sum of ______________________________ dollars ($_____________) in hand paid to the party of the first part by the party of the second part, receipt of which is hereby fully acknowledged, the party of the first part does hereby give, grant, bargain, sell, and convey unto the party of the second part, his or her heirs and assigns, all of the lot, tract, or parcel of real estate in ________________________________ Township, _______________________________ County, North Carolina, and being more particularly bounded and described as follows:

[insert full legal description].

    For a more particular description, see deed from ________________________________ to ________________________________, recorded in Deed Book _________, page _________, in the Office of the Register of Deeds of ________________________________ County.

* This item should be included in the deed when the taxing unit has assigned its bid.

This conveyance is subject to city and county property taxes for ________, the payment of which shall be assumed by the party of the second part. To have and to hold the above-described premises and all privileges and appurtenances thereunto appertaining, to the party of the second part, his or her heirs and assigns, to their only use and behoof forever free and clear of all encumbrances except all outstanding city and county taxes and all local improvement assessments against the above-described property not included in the judgment in the above-entitled cause in as full and ample manner as the party of the first part is authorized and empowered to convey the same;

** [The City of ___________________________] [_______________________ County] joins in the execution of this deed for the purpose of assigning and does hereby assign, transfer, and deliver to said party of the second part, his or her heirs and assigns, its bid to the above-described property which it made at the aforesaid public sale on the __________ day of _____________________________, ________, together with all right, title, interest, and estate in the property to which it is entitled by reason of its bid.

In witness whereof, the party of the first part has hereunto set his hand and seal, the day and year first above written.

____
                                                                        (Seal)
                                                                        Sheriff

____
                                                                        (Seal)
[Mayor of City of ___________________]
[Chair of Board of Commissioners of
_________________________________ County]

I, _____________________________, notary public in and for the county of ___________________________, do hereby certify that ______________________________, Sheriff of _______________________________ County, personally appeared before me this day and acknowledged the due execution of the foregoing deed as his or her own act and deed.

Witness my hand and official seal, this _______________________________ day of _____________________________, ________.

____
                                                                        Notary Public

My commission expires _______________________________, ________.

** This item should be included in the deed when the taxing unit has assigned its bid.

When a proper upset bid has been made, G.S. 1-339-64(f) requires the clerk of superior court to notify the sheriff, and the sheriff is then required to mail a written notice of the upset bid by first-class mail to the last known addresses of the last prior bidder and the current record owners of the property.

G.S. 1-339.64, as amended in 2001 and effective January 1, 2002, provides for successive upset bids and a resale only in the event a motion for a resale is made pursuant to G.S. 1-339.66A. The former practice of a motion for and order of resale after each upset bid has been eliminated. After ten days have expired following a sale, resale, or upset bid, without another upset bid or motion for resale, the rights of the parties become fixed and the clerk may confirm the sale pursuant to G.S. 1-339.67. If one or more upset bids has been made, the sale being confirmed is the sale based on the last upset bid. Form 14 is for the order of confirmation.

ASSIGNMENT OF BID

G.S. 105-376(a) provides that a taxing unit that has bid in the property at the foreclosure sale "may assign its bid at any time by private sale for not less than the amount of the bid." An assignment (Form 13) made by the taxing unit should be signed in the unit's name by the chief executive officer—mayor or chair of the board—and attested by the clerk of the board, with the seal affixed. Authority for making the assignment should appear in the board's minutes.

ORDER OF CONFIRMATION

G.S. 1-339.67 provides for an order of confirmation to be entered after the time for submitting an upset bid has expired. No sale may be consummated until confirmed by the clerk of the superior court.

SHERIFF'S DEED

G.S. 1-339.68 states: "Upon confirmation of a sale of real property, the sheriff upon order of the clerk of the superior court, shall prepare and tender to the purchaser a duly executed deed for the property sold and, upon compliance by the purchaser with the terms of the sale, shall deliver the deed to the purchaser." G.S. 105-375(i) provides: "The purchaser shall acquire title to the property in fee simple, free and clear of all claims, rights, interests and liens except the liens of other taxes and assessments not paid from the purchase price and not included in the judgment." Form 15 has been prepared to meet these requirements.

Note that G.S. 105-375 contains no instructions to the sheriff concerning application of funds derived from the foreclosure sale. Thus he is governed by G.S. 1-399.70:

> (a) After deducting all sums due him on account of the sale, including the expenses incurred in caring for the property so long as his responsibility for such care continued, the sheriff shall pay the proceeds of the sale to the clerk of the superior court who issued the execution, and the clerk shall furnish the sheriff a receipt therefor.
> (b) The clerk shall apply the proceeds of the sale so received to the payment of the judgment upon which the execution was issued.
> (c) Any surplus shall be paid by the clerk to the person legally entitled thereto if the clerk knows who such person is. If the clerk is in doubt as to who is entitled to the surplus, or if adverse claims are asserted thereto, the clerk shall hold such surplus until rights thereto are established in a special proceeding pursuant to G.S. § 1-339.71.

The sheriff deducts from the proceeds all mailing and publication costs, as well as his sale fees.

SHERIFF'S RETURN OF EXECUTION

After the sheriff has executed and delivered a deed to the property and has received payment from the successful bidder, he should complete the return portion of the execution (see Form 9) and deliver the completed execution to the clerk of the superior court, along with the proceeds of the sale. The sheriff's return should include (a) a statement that the property was sold; (b) the date of the sale; (c) the amount collected at the sale; (d) the amount deducted for any expenses and the sheriff's commission; and (e) the balance to be turned over to the clerk. The return should take the following form: "Execution satisfied by sale of the above-described property on the _______ day of ________________________, ______, to ____________________________, the successful bidder for $________. Of the amount of $________ collected, I have kept $________ for my commission and $______________ for expenses, and I am returning $________ with this execution."

G.S. 1-321 requires the clerk to enter the returned execution in the judgment docket opposite the entry of the judgment.

3

POST-SALE MATTERS

POST-SALE MATTERS

INTRODUCTION

Once a foreclosure sale has been completed and the property sold to either a private purchaser or the taxing unit, the tax collector and attorney confront a number of post-sale issues. The handling of these issues usually depends on whether the property was sold to a private purchaser or to the taxing unit. Several preliminary matters, however, are the same regardless of who purchased the property and whether the mortgage-style or the *in rem* procedure was used.

REMEDIES AGAINST THE TAXPAYER

One of these preliminary matters is whether the taxing unit has any remedies against the taxpayer if the property was sold at the foreclosure sale for less than the total amount of the taxes and costs. In mortgage-style foreclosures, G.S. 105-374(q)(2) expressly provides for acceptance of a bid at the sale less than the total amount of the taxes and costs. The *in rem* statutes do not provide one way or the other regarding acceptance of a bid in an amount insufficient to pay all taxes and costs, but G.S. 105-375(i) provides that the sheriff is to sell the property under the procedures for execution sales, and those procedures require that the notice of sale state that the property will be sold to the highest bidder.[1] Therefore under either procedure the taxing unit apparently may accept a bid from a private purchaser that is the highest bid for the property but is not high enough to pay all of the taxes and costs. The other choice for the taxing unit bringing the foreclosure is to enter its own bid in an amount sufficient to pay all taxes and costs. The choice it makes in situations where the private bid is insufficient usually depends on the

---

1. N.C. GEN. STAT. § 1-339.51.

amount of the bid in relation to the market value of the property: If the taxing unit believes that the private bid, though insufficient to pay all taxes and costs, is close to what the property will sell for (and thus is all the taxing unit would receive if it bid in the property at the sale and then attempted to resell the property), it should accept the private bid. If the taxing unit believes that the private bid is substantially below the market value of the property, it should probably enter its own bid in an amount sufficient to pay the taxes and costs.

If the taxing unit accepts a private bid in an amount less than the total amount of the judgment, it then faces the question asked above: May it attempt to collect the difference between the amount of the bid and the total amount of the taxes and costs from the taxpayer? The answer appears to be no, it must settle for the amount of the bid, primarily because the foreclosure judgment is a judgment *in rem*; it is not a personal judgment against the taxpayer, and only a personal judgment would give the taxing unit a right to collect a deficiency. G.S. 105-375(a) specifically provides that it is an *in rem* proceeding, and case law holds that a mortgage-style foreclosure results in an *in rem* judgment (against the property only) and not a personal judgment against the taxpayer.[2] In addition, G.S. 105-366(b) provides that once a foreclosure complaint has been filed pursuant to G.S. 105-374 or a judgment docketed pursuant to G.S. 105-375, the tax collector no longer has authority to proceed against the taxpayer's personal property by means of levy or attachment and garnishment.

EXTINGUISHING LIENS AND ACCOUNTING FOR PAYMENT

The sale of the property under foreclosure and acceptance of a bid is apparently conclusive regarding payment of the tax; that is, the taxes included in the lien or liens foreclosed must be regarded as paid, whether or not the bid was sufficient, because the judgment is satisfied and the taxing unit has no more remedies. Therefore the tax collector and finance officer should make the appropriate accounting entries to treat the tax as fully paid and no longer part of the collector's charge.

THE TAXING UNIT AS PURCHASER

If the property is sold to a private purchaser, it will be listed to the new owner, and there is nothing more for the tax collector to do as a result of the foreclosure. If, however, the taxing unit purchased the property at the

---

2. Town of Apex v. Templeton, 223 N.C. 645, 27, S.E.2d 617 (1943).

sale, it has a choice: it may either pay the total amount due, including taxes owed to other taxing units, and thereafter hold the property as sole owner, or it may pay only the costs of the foreclosure including court costs and sheriff's, commissioner's, and attorney's fees and thereafter hold the property for the benefit of any other taxing unit with liens on the property.[3] The second procedure is the one almost always followed and the one discussed here.

A taxing unit that purchases the property and chooses this second option holds the property for the benefit of other taxing units that have tax liens on the property. The purchasing unit should aggressively attempt to sell the property to a private purchaser; as long as it holds the property, it receives no payment of its taxes, and the property remains exempt from taxation. The governing board of the taxing unit may, at any time, sell the property to its former owner or to another person who had an interest in the property by private sale.[4] The former owner or other person with an interest must pay the amount of the judgment plus sale costs, plus taxes not included in the judgment, plus the taxes of other units.[5]

RESALE OF THE PROPERTY BY THE TAXING UNIT

In most cases the former owner will not purchase the property, so the taxing unit must seek another purchaser. The procedures for selling real property acquired at a foreclosure sale are the same as for selling other real property owned by the taxing unit.[6] The governing board should declare the property surplus[7] and then proceed to sell it by public auction, advertisement for sealed bids, or negotiated offer, advertisement, and upset bid.[8] The governing board determines the acceptable sales price,[9] which may be in an amount less than the total taxes and costs in the foreclosure judgment.[10] The governing board is not obligated to obtain permission for the sale from other taxing units with liens on the property.[11]

---

3. N.C. Gen. Stat. § 105-376(b).

4. Id. § 105-376(c).

5. *Id.*

6. *Id. See also* Lawrence, Local Government Property Transactions in North Carolina (Institute of Government 1987), ch. VI [hereinafter Lawrence].

7. Lawrence, at 74.

8. N.C. Gen. Stat. § 160A-266.

9. *Id.* § 105-376(c).

10. *See id.* § 105-376(b).

11. *Id.*

When the property is sold, if the sales price is less than the amount necessary to pay all taxes and costs, the sales proceeds are distributed as follows.

First, the selling unit is reimbursed for disbursements made in bringing the foreclosure action, which include court costs, attorney's, sheriff's, and commissioner's fees, postage, and publication costs.[12]

Second, the remaining balance is distributed to each taxing unit having liens on the property "in proportion" to that unit's interest.[13] This means that a ratio has to be established based on each taxing unit's interest in the property. A taxing unit's interest in the property is determined by adding

1. The taxes of the unit, with penalties, interest, and costs (other than costs already reimbursed to the purchasing unit) to satisfy which the property was ordered sold;
2. Other taxes of the unit, with penalties, interest, and costs which would have been paid in full from the purchase price had the purchase price been paid in full;
3. Taxes of the unit, with penalties, interest, and costs to which the foreclosure sale was made subject . . .[14]

Distribution of the funds can be illustrated by the following example. Taxing unit A foreclosed on a parcel of property pursuant to G.S. 105-374. The amount of A's taxes and interest included in the judgment was $2,000; the amount of costs was $500, including court costs and attorney's fees. Taxing unit B's taxes in the amount of $1,000 were also included in the judgment. At the sale, the highest private bid was $1,000, so taxing unit A made the high bid of $2,500 and became the owner of the property. Taxing unit A was required to spend $500 to pay the costs of the foreclosure. One year later, taxing unit A sells the property to a private purchaser by sealed bids for $2,000. Taxing unit A retains the first $500 in proceeds as reimbursement for its foreclosure costs; distribution of the remaining $1,500 is determined by finding the proportion of A's and B's interests in the property. A's taxes were $2,000 and B's were $1,000, a ratio of two to one, so A retains $1,000 and disburses $500 to B.

If the sale of the property by the foreclosing unit brings more than the total of taxes and costs, the excess is first applied to special assessments included in the judgment and then to special assessments to which the foreclosure sale was made subject; any money remaining after payment of special assessments is retained by the foreclosing unit.[15]

---

12. *Id.*

13. N.C. Gen. Stat. § 105-376(b).

14. *Id.*

15. *Id.*